A NEW APPROACH TO THE VEDAS

A NEW APPROACH TO THE VEDAS

BY

ANANDA K. COOMARASWAMY

GYAN

Published by

Gyan Publishing House
5, Ansari Road
Daryaganj, New Delhi-110002
Phone: 011-47034999, 9811692060
E-mail: books@gyanbooks.com

Distribution Network
gyanbooks.com
India, USA, Canada, UK, Australia

ISBN: 978-93-6280-301-6 (PB)
First Published, 1933

2nd Impression 2024

Printed at: Gyan Press, Delhi.

A NEW APPROACH TO THE VEDAS
Author: ANANDA K. COOMARASWAMY

A NEW APPROACH TO THE VEDAS

AN ESSAY IN TRANSLATION AND EXEGESIS

BY

ANANDA K. COOMARASWAMY

LONDON

LUZAC & CO.

46 GREAT RUSSELL STREET, W.C. 1

1933

CONTENTS

INTRODUCTION

Existing translations of Vedic texts, however etymologically "accurate," are too often unintelligible or unconvincing, sometimes admittedly unintelligible to the translator himself. Neither the "Sacred Books of the East," nor for example such translations of the Upaniṣads as those of R. E. Hume, or those of Mitra, Roer, and Cowell, recently reprinted, even approach the standards set by such works as Thomas Taylor's version of the *Enneads* of Plotinus, or Friedländer's of Maimonides' *Guide for the Perplexed*. Translators of the Vedas do not seem to have possessed any previous knowledge of metaphysics, but rather to have gained their first and only notions of ontology from Sanskrit sources. As remarked by Jung, *Psychological Types*, p. 263, with reference to the study of the Upaniṣads under existing conditions, "any true perception of the quite extraordinary depth of those ideas and their amazing psychological accuracy is still but a remote possibility."

It is very evident that for an understanding of the Vedas, a knowledge of Sanskrit, *however profound*, is insufficient. Indians themselves do not rely upon their knowledge of Sanskrit here, but insist upon the absolute necessity of study at the feet of a *guru*. That is not possible in the same sense for European students. Yet Europe also possesses a tradition founded in first principles. That mentality which in the twelfth and thirteenth centuries brought into being an intellectual Christianity owing as much to Maimonides, Aristotle,[1] and the Arabs as to the Bible itself, would not have found the Vedas "difficult." For example, those who understood that "Paternity and filiation . . . are *dependent* properties," or that God "cannot be a Person without a Nature, nor can his Nature be without a Person," Eckhart, I, 268 and 394,[2] or had read later Dante's "O Virgin Mother, daughter of thy Son," *Paradiso*, xxxiii, would not have seen in the mutual generation of Puruṣa and Virāj, or Dakṣa and Aditi an arbitrary or primitive mode of thought: those familiar with Christian conceptions of Godhead as "void," "naked," and "as though it were not," would not have been disconcerted by descriptions of That as "Death" (*mṛtyu*), and as being "in no wise" (*neti, neti*). To those who even to-day have some idea of what is meant by a "reconciliation of opposites," or have partly understood the relation between man's conscious consciousness and the *unconscious* sources of his powers, the significance of the Waters as an "inexhaustible well" of the possibilities of existence might be apparent. When Blake speaks of a "Marriage of Heaven and Hell," or Swinburne writes, "I bid you but be," there is included more of the Vedas than can be found in many learned disquisitions on their "philosophy." What right have Sanskritists to confine their labours to the solution of linguistic problems: is it fear that precludes their wrestling with the ideology of the text they undertake? Our scholarship is too little humane.[3]

What I have called here a "new approach to the Vedas" is nothing more than an essay in the exposition of Vedic ideas by means of a translation and a commentary in which the resources of other forms of the universal tradition are taken for granted. Max Müller, in 1891, held that the Veda would continue to occupy scholars "for centuries to come." Meanwhile there are others beside professional scholars, for whom the Vedas are significant. In any case, no great extension of our present measure of understanding can be expected from philological research alone, however valuable such methods of research may have been in the past: and what is true for Sumero-Babylonian religion is no less true for the Vedas, viz., that

" further progress in the interpretation of the difficult cycle of . . . liturgies cannot be made until the cult is more profoundly interpreted from the point of view of the history of religion."[4]

As regards the translation: every English word employed has been used advisedly with respect to its technical significance. For example, " nature " is here always the correlative of " essence," and denoted that whereby the world is *as* it is ; never as in modern colloquial usage to denote the world, *ens naturata.* Similarly, existence is distinguished from being, creation from emanation, local movement from the principle of motion, the incalculable from the infinite, and so forth. All that is absolutely necessary if the sense of the Vedic texts is to be conveyed. In addition, the few English words added to complete the sense of the translation are italicised : and when several English words are employed to render one Sanskrit term, the English words are generally connected by hyphens, e.g., Āditya, " Supernal-Sun " ; Akṣara, " Imperishable-Word."

As regards the commentary : here I have simply used the resources of Vedic and Christian scriptures side by side. An extended use of Sumerian, Taoist, Ṣūfī, and Gnostic sources would have been at once possible and illuminating, but would have stretched the discussion beyond reasonable limits.[5] As for the Vedic and Christian sources, each illuminates the other. And that is in itself an important contribution to understanding, for as Whitman expresses it, " These are really the thoughts of all men in all ages and lands, they are not original with me. If they are not yours as much as mine, they are nothing, or next to nothing." Whatever may be asserted or denied with respect to the " value " of the Vedas, this at least is certain, that their fundamental doctrines are by no means singular.

ANANDA K. COOMARASWAMY.

Museum of Fine Arts, Boston, *December*, 1932.

I

BṚHADĀRAṆYAKA UPANIṢAD, I, 2
(= Śatapatha Brāhmaṇa X, 6, 5)

In the beginning (*agre*) no thing whatsoever was here. This-all (*idam*) was veiled by Death (*mṛtyu*), by Privation (*aśanāyā*) : for Privation is Death. That (*tad*) took-on (*akuruta*) Intellect (*manas*), " Let me be Selfed " (*ātmanvī syām*). He (*saḥ*), *Self*, manifested Light (*arcan acarat*). Of Him, as he shone, were the Waters (*āpaḥ*) born (*jāyanta*). " Verily, whilst I shone, there was Delight " (*kam*), said-He (*iti*). This is the Sheen (*arkatva*) of Shining (*arka*). Verily, there is delight for him who knoweth thus the sheen of shining. 1.

Our text deals with the origin of Light from Darkness, Life from Death, Actuality from Possibility, Self from the Un-selfed, *saguṇa* from *nirguṇa* Brahman, " I am " from Unconsciousness, God from Godhead. " The first formal assumption in Godhead is being . . . God," Eckhart, I, 267. " The Nothing bringeth itself into a Will," Böhme, *XL Questions concerning the Soule*, I, 178 : " an eternal will arises in the nothing, to introduce the nothing into something, that the will might find, feel, and behold itself," *Signatura Rerum*, I, 8. " The Tao became One," *Tao Tê Ching*, II, 42.[6]

Compare *Taittirīya Up.*, II, 7 *svayam akurut' ātmānam* " of itself assumed Self," and *svayambhū*, " self-become,"

Upaniṣads *passim* : *Maitri Up.*, V, 2 and II, 5, " In the beginning this world was a Dark-Inert (*tamas*) . . . that proceeds to differentiation (*viṣamatva*) . . . even as the awakening of a sleeper." That is Eckhart's " passive welling up " : " the beginning of the Father is primary, not proceeding," " the Father is the manifestation of the Godhead," I, 268, 267 and 135. Just as also, microcosmically, " Without a doubt, consciousness is derived from the unconscious " (Wilhelm and Jung).

Now as to " One " : an intelligible distinction can be made between the inconnumerable Unity of God " without a second," the Sameness of Godhead, and the Identity, Deity, of God and Godhead, *mūrta* and *amūrta* Brahman : " between the pillars of the conscious and unconscious . . . all beings and all worlds," Kabīr, Bolpur ed., II, 59 ; " One and One uniting, there is the Supreme Being," Eckhart, I, 368. That these are here " rational, not real " distinctions (Eckhart, I, 268) appears in the fact that " One " can be spoken equally of Unity, Sameness, and Identity : God, Godhead, Deity, is not a distinction of Persons. On the other hand, " One " cannot be said of the Trinity as such. These distinctions, necessarily and clearly made in exegesis, when literally interpreted, become definitions of sectarian points of view, theistic, nihilistic, and metaphysical[7] : in *bhakti-vāda* the Unity, in *śūnya-vāda* the Sameness, in *jñāna-vāda* the Identity are respectively *paramārthika*, ultimately significant. In Śākta cults there survives an ontology antedating patriarchal modes of thought, and the relation of the conjoint principles is reversed (*viparita*) in gender : here Śiva, inert, effecting nothing by himself, represents the Godhead, while Śakti, Mother of All Things, is the active power, engendering, preserving, and resolving, *līlā* is not " his " but " hers." In " mysticism " there is an emotional realisation of all or any of these points of view. In reality, " the path men take from every side is Mine," *Bhagavad Gītā*, IV, 11 ; " In whatever way you find God best and are most aware of him that way pursue," Eckhart, I, 482.

It should be observed further that while we speak in theology[8] of First, Second, and Third Persons, the Persons being connected (*bandhu*, *Ṛg Veda*, X, 129, 4, *Bṛhadāraṇyaka Up.*, I, 1, 2) by opposite relation,[9] the numerical ordering of the Persons is purely conventional (*saṁketita*), not a chronological or real order of coming into being: for the Persons are connascent, *itaretarajanmāna*, the Trinity (*tridhā*) is an arrangement (*saṁhitā*), not a process. For example, the Son creates the Father as much as the Father the Son,[10] for there can be no paternity without a filiation, and *vice versa*, and that is what is meant by "opposite relation." Similarly, there cannot be a Person (Puruṣa) without Nature (Prakṛti), and *vice versa*. That is why in metaphysical "mythology" we meet with "inversions," as for example, when in the *Ṛg Veda*, X, 72, 4, Dakṣa (a personal name of the Progenitor, see *Śatapatha Brāhmaṇa*, II, 4, 4, 2) is born of Aditi as her son, and she also of him as his daughter; or X, 90, 5, where Virāj is born of Puruṣa, and *vice versa*. Metaphysics are consistent, but not systematic: system is found only in religious extensions,[11] where a given ordering of the Persons becomes a dogma, and it is precisely by such "matters of faith," and not by a difference of metaphysical basis, that one religion is distinguished from another. That is truly a "distinction without a difference."

It should be observed that the connascence (*sahajanma*) of Father-essence and Mother-nature, the "two forms" of Brahman, though metaphorically spoken of as "birth" (*janma*), is not a sexual-begetting, not a generation from conjoint principles, *maithunya prajanana*: in that sense both are equally un-begotten, un-born, as in *Śvetāśvatara Up.*, I, 8, *dvāvajau*, or as implied in the *Bṛhadāraṇyaka Up.*, I, 4, 3 where the origination of the conjoint principles called a "falling apart," diremption, or karyokinesis, *dvedhā-pāta.* "One became Two," viz., Yin and Yang, *Tao Tê Ching*, II, 42.

On the other hand, their common Son, Agni Brahmā-Prajāpati, etc., being consubstantial with the Spirit (*prâṇa*)[12] is at once unborn in the same sense, *and* born by a generation from the conjoint principles.[13] Only the latter birth can be thought of as an "event" taking place at the dawn of a creative cycle, in the beginning, *agre.*

With respect to *kam,* "Delight," "Affirmation": Will (*kāma*) or Fiat (*syād*) are the moving power (*dakṣa, rerivā*) in all procession (*krama, prasaraṇa*), *kāma* is the will-to-life, "so great indeed is *kāma*," *Bṛhadāraṇyaka Up.*, I, 4, 17. Will, *kāma,* is an essential name of God; it is by his Will that his intrinsic-form (*svarūpa*) signs and seals intrinsic-nature (*svabhāva*), Nature for her part desiring form. So the single Will in Deity may be regarded from two points of view, with respect to essence as the Will-spirit, and with respect to nature as the Craving[14]: as Gandharva and Apsaras (= Urvaśī, *Ṛg Veda*, VII, 33, 11, and Apyā, X, 13, 4, Kāmadeva and Ratī, Eros I, 8, 20 and 33, where Nārâyaṇa is "love" (*kāma, lobha, rāga*) and Śrī-Lakṣmī is "desire" (*icchā, tṛṣṇā, ratī*).

These two aspects of the Will are plainly seen in the Vedic "legend" of the Birth of Vasiṣṭha,[15] and the *Pañcaviṁśa Brāhmaṇa* passage cited below, p. 8. In the first case Mitra-Varuṇau is quite literally seduced by the fascinations of the Apsaras Urvaśī; in the second, the Waters are literally "in heat." God thus affirms himself because it is his nature so to come forth: existence is his knowledge of himself, that is his eating of the fruit of the tree, for to eat is to exist. In other words, the possibility of existence necessarily involves the fact of existence: that is precisely His omnipotence who is without (unrealised) potentialities and is never idle though he never works. Nor does he act unwittingly, he drinks the poison (*viṣa*) and objectivity (*viṣamata*) of existence as well as its delights; whereby his throat is scorched and blackened.

It will be seen that no real distinction can be drawn in principle between the Fall of God and that of Man : both are the necessary consequences of a divine nature common to both. The sin and shame, the virtue and glory of existence are his as much as ours.[16] The difference between us is that he knowingly remains within at the same time that he comes forth Self-ishly, we are conscious *only* in our "self." He is a tide at once fontal and inflowing : we are its waves, oblivious that wave is water too. Our only error is to see distinction here : the Comprehensor, *ya evaṁ vidvān*, knowing himself no more as wave, but as the sea him-Self, returns with the tide to its source, which neither he nor the Supreme Self have ever really, but only logically, left.

The Will proceeds as Love, "by way of the Will as Love," St. Thomas, Sum. Th., I, Q. 36, A. 2 ; that "mutual outpouring of love . . . is the common spiration of the Father and the Son," Eckhart, I, 269. "We desire a thing while as yet we do not possess it. When we have it, we love it, desire then falling away," Eckhart, I, 82[17] : but as there is nothing that he does not possess in himself, who does not proceed from potentiality to act, but is all act, his will is his love, "Eternity is in love with the productions of time," Blake, cf. *Ṛg Veda*, VII, 87, 2. That is his affirmation and delight, *kam*, *ānanda*, "God enjoys himself in all things . . . finding his reflection most delightful," Eckhart, I, 243 and 425, cf. *pramudaṁ prayāti*, Śaṅkarâcārya, *Svâtmanirūpaṇa*, 95.

Veda neither asserts a beginning in time, nor a creation *ex nihilo*.[18] "In the beginning" does not mean "at a given time," nor eventfully, but in an ever-present now, of which empirical experience is impossible, human knowledge being only of the past, and human expectation only of the future : *agre* is first in order, primordial, *in principio*, rather than first in time. "In the beginning, this world was merely Water," *Bṛhadāraṇyaka Up.*, V, 5, 1 : that is to say all the possibilities of existence, not yet existence, but not an impossibility of existence, a true nothing, to be compared to the horns of a hare or the son of a barren woman. To say that the world was not, that there was no thing, or as in Genesis that all was " without form and void," is not to say that nothing was. What was is called *pradhāna*, *mūla-prakṛti*, the Waters, Dark-Inert (*tamas*), and by many other names : what was not is the world, life, existence, multiplicity, variety, *ens naturata*, the Three Worlds.

As to the conception of Godhead in our text : Mṛtyu, Death, is lifelessness, and lifelessness, in the technical phraseology of St. Thomas, is " lack of an intrinsic form," Sum. Th., II, Q. 6, A. 2. " A prodigy, and is not being . . . (but) prior to motion and prior to intelligence," Plotinus, *Enneads*, VI, 9, 6. So the Godhead, Death-absolute,[19] is also called Privation : for " That " is " the unexpounded (*anirukta*), invisible (*adṛśya*), not-selfed, (*anātmya*), placeless (*anilayana*) ground (*pratiṣṭhā*)," *Taittirīya Up.*, II, 7. " Nothing true can be spoken of God," " God is neither this nor that," " Know'st thou of him anything ? He is no such thing," Eckhart, I, 87, 211, and 246 : " which hath no ground or byss to stand on, and where there is no place to dwell in . . . it may fitly be compared to nothing," Böhme, *Supersensual Life*. Such a negative manner of speaking is inevitable : for here negation, *neti*, *neti*,[20] " not so, not thus," is a denial of limiting conditions, a double negative ; not as with us, who " make innate denial " that we are other than ourselves, an affirmation of limiting conditions. So Godhead is " void," " light and darkness, it is rid of both," " poised in itself in sable stillness," it is " idle," " effects neither this nor that," is " as poor, as naked, and as empty as though it were not ; it has not, wills not, wants not," " motionless dark," Eckhart, I, 267-270, 368, 369, 381.[21]

Aśanāyā, want, is privation of " food," the means of existence. So in the language of the Upaniṣads, " to eat food," *annam ad*, is to "live," "exist," "function," "energise," "be mode-ified" (*-maya*), or "natured." In distinction from Godhead, Death, God lives, for all things are his "food." So "food is the supreme form (*rūpa*) of the Self, food the mode (*-maya*) of the Spirit (*prâṇa*, here "breath of life") . . . from food are the begotten (*prajāḥ*) born (*prajāyante*) . . . by food they live (*jīvanti*), and thereto they return at last," *Maitri Up.*, VI, 11: and "it is even He manifested Light": "motionless dark . . . this darkness is the incomprehensible nature of God . . . first to arise in it is Light . . . (and) this supremely pure splendour of the impartible essence illumines all things at once . . . the patent of his power, resplendent in luminous detail," Eckhart, I, 369, 373, 366, 399. Or as our text expresses it, of him, as he shone, were the Waters "born," that is precisely "brought to light"; "He illumines (*bhāsayati*) these worlds . . . incarnadines (*rañjayati*) existences here," *Maitri Up.*, VI, 7.

"For him who knoweth thus," *ya evaṁ vidvān*, Comprehensor: with this constant refrain the Upaniṣads invariably introduce a statement of the immediate and the transcendental values of the knowledge previously imparted. Just as Eckhart, for example, after describing the procession of the Spirit as Life, "it is flowing from the Spirit and is altogether ghostly, and in this power God comes out in the full flower of his joy and glory, as he is in himself," adds "were he always recollected in this power a man would never age," I, 291; or in the words of Böhme, "The magician has power in this Mystery," *Sex Puncta Mystica*, VI, 2. Professor Edgerton has admirably demonstrated how the Vedas are never in search of knowledge for its own sake, but inasmuch as Understanding is thought of as synonymous with plenitude, power, and freedom.[22]

The Waters, verily, were a counter-shining

(*arka*). What was the foam (*śara*) of the Waters, that solidified, that became Earth (*pṛthivī*). Thereon He, *Self,* strove (*aśrāmayat*). The Fiery-Energy (*tejas*) and the Tincture (*rasa*) of his striving (*śrānta*) and intension (*tapta*) broke forth (*niravartat*) as Fire (*agni*). 2.

The "first day of creation" is thus described as the reflection (*ābhāsa*) of a light-image (*bhā-rūpa*) in the mirror of the as yet undifferentiated possibilities of existence: that is the Sheen of Shining, *arkasya arkatva,* Dante's "suo splendore . . . risplendendo," *Paradiso,* XXIX, 14 and 15.[23] Cf. *Ṛg Veda,* X, 82, 5 and 6, where the Several Angels are seen together (*samapaśyanta*) in One Projection (*arpitam*)[24] from the navel of the Unborn (i.e., Varuṇa) as he lies germinal (*garbha*), recumbent (*uttānapad*) on the surface of the Waters: and *Pañcaviṁśa Brāhmaṇa,* VII, 8, 1: "Unto the Waters came their season. The Spirit stirred their back, therefrom became a fair-thing, Mitra-Varuṇau counter-saw (*paryapaśyata*) themselves therein." "He shines upon this world in the form of man," *imaṁ lokamabhyārcat puruṣarūpeṇa, Aitareya Āraṇyaka,* II, 2, 1. So in Genesis, "the Spirit of God moved on the face of the Waters," and "He created man in his own image": "by this reflection of his divine nature the intellect of the Father fashions or utters itself . . . his light, his flowing intellect to wit, was shining on this world-stuff wherein the world subsisted in the Father in uncreated formless simplicity," Eckhart, I, 397 and 404: "And this is the Image and Likeness of God, and our Image and our Likeness; for in it God reflects Himself and all things," Ruysbroeck, *Adornment of the Spiritual Marriage,* III,[25] Dante, "La gloria di colui che tutto move per l'universo penetra e risplende," and "quella circulazion, che si concetta pareva in te come lume riflesso . . . mi parve pinta della nostra effige," *Paradiso*, I, 1-2, and XXXIII, 127-131.

" For that God *is* God he gets from creatures," and " I have loved you in the reflection of my darkness," the " reflection of the mirror in the sun is in the sun," Eckhart, I, 274, 377 and 143 : " as when a man beholdeth his face in a mirror," Böhme, *Clavis*, 42 and 43. Or from Indian sources, " Without Thee I have no intrinsic-form, without me Thou hast no existence," *Siddhântamuktâvalī*, lii ; " without Śiva no Devī, without Devī no Śiva," *Kāmakalāvilāsa*, Commentary, citing *āgama* with reference to the text, 2, " She is the pure mirror wherein Śiva sees his own intrinsic-form."[26] This conception of the relativity of God, Böhme's " Gegenwurf," which we might call a *prakāśa-vimarṣa-vāda*, " doctrine of light and reflection," and implies that the Fire that shines forth as Light is a *dark* heat until and simultaneously illuminated by the counter-shining, leads to developments of fundamental significance. That God is man-made, " takes the forms imagined by his worshippers " (*Kailāya-malai*, Ceylon National Review, Jan., 1907, p. 285), that his forms " are determined by the relation that subsists between the worshipped and the worshipper " (*Śukranītisāra*, IV, 4, 159), gives man the right to worship him in any guise whereby he is most aware of him and denies man's right to speak of any " other " gods as " false."

The Waters and the Earth are to be understood not only with reference to our terrestrial seas and continents, but as respectively the possibilities of existence in any of the Three Worlds, and the support of living beings existent in any one of them according to the terms of its possibilities : in other words, the " Waters " are literally *peut être*, *bhaviṣya*, the Earth any corresponding plane or sphere (*loka*, *dhātu*, *kṣetra*, *bhūmi*) or support (*pratiṣṭhā*) of experience[27]: and any such Earth floats like a lotus, or like foam, or like a ship, on the surface of the Waters in which it is established. The movement of the Spirit by which the Waters are stirred is not in itself a local movement, but local in effect, so that the surface of the Waters is thrown into waves, and thereby the reflection of the Light is multiplied, contracted and identified into variety. *Aitareya Āraṇyaka*, II, 1, 7, "As far as the Waters extend as far as Varuṇa extends, so far extends His world," asserts the fundamental doctrine of the identity of "possible" and "real."

The striving and intension are not easy to explain: both imply conation, the latter (*tapas*) is precisely Hebrew *ẓimẓum*. *Tapas* is not a penance, because not expiatory, but rather an anguish and a passion: a dark heat of the consciousness, a kindling not yet a flame, or to take an analogy from Physics, a raising of potential to the sparking point.[28] Notions of a smouldering continence and intellectual fermentation, as well as of a vegetative incubation, are implied. *Tejas* and *rasa* are forms of energy, respectively fiery and fluid: *tejas* the fire of love and wrath, *rasa* the elixir, tincture, or water of life. *Tejas* as element corresponds in part to "phlogiston."

"Broke forth as Fire": for "the Eternal Father is manifested in the fire . . . this *flagrat* is effected in the enkindling of the fire in the essence of the anguish," Böhme, *Signatura Rerum*, XIV, 38 and 31, "with the enkindling of the fire in the salnitral flagrat two kingdoms separate, viz., eternity and time," *ibid.*, VII, 8, cf. "the fire itself, viz., the first principle in the life, with which the light and dark world do separate," *ibid.*, IV, 8. Also "A third master has said that God is a fire. He too speaks truly, though in a likeness. For Fire is the noblest in nature and mightiest in operation amongst the elements it never rests until it reaches heaven. It is much wider and higher than Air, Water, or Earth, it comprehends all other elements in itself," Eckhart, from Büttner's *Schriften und Predigten*, 1923, II, p. 144.

Agni, "Fire," appears in the Vedic liturgies as the

preferred designation of the First-manifested Principle, on the one hand because of the fiery nature of the Supernal-Sun, and on the other because of the primary importance of fire in the sacrificial ritual. In our text (2 and 3) the divine Fire is alluded to from two different points of view, first as an undivided principle, as also specifically in *Ṛg Veda*, I, 69, 1, where Agni is the "Father of the Angels" and V, 3, 1, where Agni is Varuṇa "at birth," and Mitra "when enkindled," "in Him" are the Several Angels, and He is Indra to the mortal worshipper: and second, as one member of the Trinity of Agni, Āditya, Vāyu. The latter Agni, the Son of God, is commonly called Vaiśvānara, "Universal," with reference to his manifestation in the terrestrial, intermediate, and celestial regions; and is pre-eminently "First-born" and "Youngest" because perpetually brought to birth in the sacrificial fire at the dawn of every temporal cycle and the dawn of every day.

In any case, it is an elemental Fiery Energy (*tejas*) that underlies and typifies all other manifestation: so in procession, "the Fiery-energy (*tejas*), intrinsic-form of the firmament, in the vacance of the inner man, determined as the Trinity of Fire, Supernal-Sun, and Spirit, three factors of the Imperishable-Word, OṀ, sprouts forth, springs up, and suspires (or blossoms)" as a Burning Bush, the all-pervading Tree of Life, *Maitri Up*, see pp. 48-51. With this compare Isaiah, XI, 1, 2, *Egredietur virga de radice Jesse et flos de radice ejus ascendet et requiescet super eum spiritus domini*, and Eckhart's Commentary, "Root of Jesse is a term for the fiery nature of God. . . . Jesse means a fire and a burning; it signifies the ground of divine love and also, the ground of the soul. Out of this ground the rod grows, i.e., in the purest and highest; it shoots up out of this virgin soil at the breaking forth of the Son. Upon the rod opens a flower, the flower of the Holy Ghost," I, 153, 154, 302.[29] Likewise Böhme, "The entire man is in his being the three worlds. The soul's centre, viz., the root of the soul's fire contains the dark-world ; and the soul's fire contains the first Principle as the true fire-world. And the noble image, or the tree of divine growth, which is generated from the soul's fire and buds forth through fierce wrathful death in freedom or in the world of light, contains the light-world or the second Principle. And the body, which in the beginning was created out of the mixed substance which at creation arose from the light-world, the dark-world, and the fire-world contains the outer world or the third mixed Principle," *Sex Puncta Mystica*, V, 28 : here the first, second, and third Principles correspond to the Trinity of Fire, Supernal-Sun, and Spirit, and the properties, *tamas*, *sattva*, and *rajas*.

Rasa is the sappy vegetative life in trees and plants, a tincture in rain, the elixir of life, the *soma*- dew that drips from the world-tree, seed in all that reproduce their kind, savour in all things eaten or drunk, and the principle of beauty in art. *Rasa* is the fertilising (*raitasa*) energy, the "flowing" intellect, as for example in *Ṛg Veda*, I, 164, 8, where Mother-Earth, partaking of Father-Heaven, is "pervaded by the tincture" (*rasā nividdhā*), and the Calf (= Agni) is begotten. "I understand here the virtual salt in the vegetable life," Böhme, *Signatura Rerum*, IX, 22. Cf. the Stoic *Logos spermatikos*.

He effected in himself a Trinity (*tridhā*) : *one third Fire* (*agni*), one third Supernal-Sun (*āditya*), one third Wind (*vāyu*).

He is verily, the Spirit (*prâṇa*), determined (*vihita*) in a Trinity : *of the Three Worlds, in the likeness of a horse.* His head the eastern (*prācī*) airt, his fore-legs that and that airt on either side. Likewise his tail the western (*pratīcī*) airt, his hinder-legs that and that airt on either side. His flanks the south and north. His back the heavens (*dyu*), his belly firmament (*antarikṣa*), his underneath this *ground*. He is established (*pratiṣṭha*) in the Waters. He who knoweth this is established wherever he may be. 3.

"A Trinity," that is as the principle of Fire in any Earth, of Light in any Heaven, of Motion in any Firmament. This basic angelic Trinity of three Principles or Persons is constantly lauded, continually referred to in the Vedas and Upaniṣads.[30] "One of them (i.e., Agni) scythes when the year-of-time is done; one of them (i.e., Āditya) with his powers surveys the worlds; of one of them (i.e., Vāyu) his sweep is seen, but not his likeness," *Ṛg Veda*, I, 164, 44. *Maitri Up.*, IV, 5-6, may be cited: "Fire (*agni*), Wind (*vāyu*) and Supernal-Sun (*āditya*)—Food (*anna*), Spirit (*prâṇa*), Time (*kāla*)—Rudra, Brahmā, Viṣṇu . . . these are the primary embodiments (*tanu*) of the transcendental (*para*) incorporeal (*aśarīra*) . . . Brahman." Cf. "Now then fire is the first cause of life; and light is the second cause; and the spirit is the third cause, and yet there is but one essence . . . which manifesteth itself," Böhme, *XL Questions concerning the Soule*, I, 276.

Now with respect to the three Persons of this Trinity: Āditya is the Supernal-Sun,[31] the "Golden Person" in the Sun, immediate source of image-bearing light (*sarūpa jyoti*), consubstantial with the real and imageless (*amūrta, nirābhāsa*) Brahman, who is very Light (*jyoti*), for "that Light is the same as the Supernal-Sun," *Maitri Up.*, VI, 3; the personal name is Viṣṇu, *sattva*-natured, for he keeps things in being. Vāyu, Wind, is the Self hypostasised as the Breath of Life, consubstantial with Brahman, Spiritus, *prâṇa*, whose breath is in himself, unsuspired (*avāta*, *Ṛg Veda*, X, 129, 2), despirated (Buddhist *nirvāta*)[32]: here the personal name is Brahmā

(Prajāpati,[33] etc.) who is *rajas*-natured, being the progenitive Person, who gives to every existence its extension in space. Agni is here specifically the fiery nature, sometimes called the Wrath of God, the devourer and transformer of all existences: whose personal name is Rudra, Śiva, *tamas*-natured, for all change is a dying, a going forth of individual form into the dark night of non-existence. At the same time this Trinity is One Being, to whom as such either of these personal names can be directly applied; the functions are described, rather than divided in the Persons. "Albeit separately lauded, these three Lords of the World are of one Self-hood and a common Nature" (*Bṛhad Devatā*, I, 70-74): that unity of the Several Angels is Agni (*Ṛg Veda*, V, 3, 1); or any one member of the Trinity may stand for all, as when in *Ṛg Veda*, I, 115, 1, the Supernal-Sun (Sūrya) is called the Self of the Universe, or Vāyu similarly in X, 168, 4.[34]

Prâṇa, Spiritus, Pneuma, Life (Taoist *ch'i*, Islamic *rūḥ*) is an essential name of the Self, as Father or as Son: not as in Christian theology, a distinct Person, though in every other respect equivalent to the "Holy Ghost." In procession, by way of the Will as the principle of Motion, *prâṇa* is often spoken of as *vāta* or *vāyu*, Wind or Air: and as the breaths of life in all existences, the Spirit becomes manifold, particularly fivefold (*Aitareya Āraṇyaka*, II, 3, 3, *Taittirīya Up.*, I, 7, *Śvetâśvatara Up.*, I, 5, etc.).

Prâṇa, Vāyu, Vāta, is that Gale of the Spirit which begins to blow at the dawn of every cycle of manifestation: thereby the glassy surface of the Waters is thrown into waves, each one of which reflects the Supernal-Sun, creating a multifarious Sheen or counter-shining, which is the world-picture. That dawn wind is not specifically mentioned in our text, but implied in the mention of the Spirit, and when it is said that the Earth becomes from the foam of the Waters.[35] Hence arises one of the fundamental problems of theology, "Why does the dawn wind of creation blow, and why *as* it blows?" We say *akāmayat*, "by the Will of God," but that is more of a description than an answer. For his Will is not an arbitrary will, an accident of being, as though He needed anything, but inevitable and essential: as Eckhart expresses it, "think not that it is with God as with a human carpenter, who works or works not as he chooses, who can do or leave undone at his good pleasure. It is not thus with God . . . He must do, willy-nilly," I, 23 and 263, cf. *Saddharma Puṇḍarīka*, XV (prose), "the Tathāgata does what-must-be-done," *kartavyaṁ karoti*. God's idiosyncrasy are both eternal work and eternal rest. He cannot do otherwise than he does: for his omnipotence does not extend to a capacity for being any other or any less than he is, he cannot make that which has been not to have been, for all that has been is in and of himself, and all the future is.[36]

It is not too hard to understand that "God's will to the creature was only one, viz., a general manifestation of the spirit," Böhme, *Signatura Rerum*, XVI, 25, Swinburne's "Thou biddst me but be." But the gift of life, "in its explication and manifestation it goes forth from eternity to eternity into two essences, viz., into evil and to good," Böhme, *ibid.*, 20; no manifestation (*vyañjana*) is conceivable except in terms of pairs of opposites, *dvandvau*. But how is the distribution of good and evil in the world determined? That is a knotty problem, for we cannot imagine the eternal energy as having predilection or as playing favourites amongst the figures of its puppet show: nor on the other hand that anything existent has come to be just what it is by mere chance, "existence" and "causality" being connascent concepts of the intellect.

Perhaps to our surprise we shall find that the problem has been treated similarly by Hindu and Christian theologians. Indian tradition, in all its forms, maintains that the individual alone is responsible for all the good or evil that befalls him; he gets, as we say colloquially, just what is coming to him, he "asks for it." As expressed in the *Aitareya Āraṇyaka*, II, 3, 2, *yathāprajñaṁ hi sambhavāḥ*, "they are born according to the measure of their understanding," cf. *Kauṣītaki Up.*, I, 2, *yathāvidyam*. "Time, intrinsic nature, necessity, accident, the elements, and ancestry (*yoni, puruṣa*) may be posited (as causes of natural species); but inasmuch as the nature of Self is not a combination of these, the Self is not the Ruler (*īśa*) of the cause of pleasure and pain . . . that Self which takes on every form is not also the shaper of forms," *Śvetâśvatara Up.*, I, 2 and 9. So the *Chāndogya Up.*, VIII, 1, 4, points out that begotten existences (*prajāḥ*) get their deserts *anuśāsana* (lit. "according to what is decreed," *śāsana* having here the force of "natural law," the "law of heaven," *dharma, ṛta*): inasmuch as the individual existences live-dependent-on (*upajīvanti*) their such and such desired ends (*yaṁ yamantam-abhikāmaḥ*). Similarly in our Upaniṣad, IV. 4, 5-7, and 22, summarised, "according to a man's works, which are actuated by his will, good or evil, as the case may be, and though he may attain his ends, he must return again from the other world to this world: he only who is without desire, whose desire is fulfilled, whose desire is him-Self, reaches Brahman, there neither right nor wrong that he may have done affect him": he escapes there from merit and demerit, *puṇya-pāpa, dharmâdharmau*.

Similarly Śaṅkarâcārya, *Vedânta Sūtra*, II, 1, 32-35, Commentary, maintains that injustice cannot be charged to Brahman, for as much as he does not act independently, but with regard to (*sāpekṣa*) merit and demerit (*dharmâdharmau*): he being the common cause of the becoming of all things, but not of the distinctions between them, which distinctions are determined by the "varying works inherent in the respective personalities."[37]

Quite or nearly in accord with this, St. Thomas, distinguishing Fate from Providence, says that it is "manifest that fate is in the created causes themselves," *Sum. Th.*, I, Q. 116, A. 2. Böhme is even more definite: "as is the harmony, viz., the life's form in each thing, so is also the sound or tone of the eternal voice therein; in the holy, holy, in the perverse perverse," and that is determined by the *turba* "which Adam took in by his imagination" and which comes into the world with every individual form of the spirit, "hanging to it," "therefore no creature can blame its creator, as if he made it evil," *Signatura Rerum*, XVI, 6 and 7, and *XL Questions concerning the Soule*, VIII, 14. Compare also Dante *Paradiso*, XVII, 37-42, "Contingency, that does not extend beyond the page of your material, is all depicted in the eternal aspect; though it takes not its necessity therefrom, no more than does a ship as it floats down the stream (depend upon) that image wherein she is mirrored."

All that follows naturally from the conclusion that neither good nor evil can have, as such, any place in pure being: that point of view, is so constantly maintained in the Upaniṣads, *Bhagavad Gītā*, and in Buddhism, that the citation of a couple of passages will amply suffice. He, Brahman, is "other than right and wrong" (*dharmâdharmau*), and "when a mortal has rent away what is rightful (*dharmya*) and receives Him as undimensioned (*anu*), then he rejoices," *Kaṭha Up.*, II, 13 and 14: "The Lord of the world emanates neither agency nor actions, nor the conjunction of action and reward, but it is each thing's nature that operates.[37a] The Lord accepts neither the ill nor the well-done of any man," *Bhagavad Gītā*, V. 14-15. In Christianity, besides that "He makes his sun to shine alike upon the just and the unjust," we find uncompromising words in Eckhart: "I must let go virtue if I would see God face to face," "God is neither good nor true," "the vision of God transcends virtues," "joys and sorrows are not sown in the ground of eternal truth," there there is "no trace of vice or virtue"; "there is nothing free but the first cause," I, 144, 272, 273, 467, 374, 146. Were it otherwise, He could not be spoken of as "just." So the dawn wind of creation must be thought of as of a double origin: one of the Spirit, moving without motion or any why, the other actuated by and because of past events.

It is not proposed to discuss here in any detail the doctrine of reincarnation, *punar apādana, punar āvṛtti.* We shall take it for granted that in its original and pure form[38] this doctrine simply implied a return from angelic to corporeal existence, in-accordance-with-a-natural-law (*śāsita, ṛtvya, dharmya*)[39] affecting all those who have not by gnosis (*jñāna, vidyā*) already achieved a total emancipation (*ati-mukti*), nor embarked on the angelic voyage (*devayāna*) of progressive emancipation (*krama mukti*), and so have neither escaped, nor are in the way to escape from the bondage of desirous works (*kāmya karma*) which are the determinants of merit and demerit (*dharmâ-dharmau, puṇya-pāpa*). We take it for granted also, what is perhaps less certain, that the return (*punar āvartana, avasarpaṇa,* etc.) was originally conceived as taking place not immediately, but in another aeon, and under a new dispensation: either in another *manvantara,* or *yuga,* or *kalpa,* or even in another *para* with the resurrection of the cosmic horse, the birth of another Brahmā-Prajāpati.[40]

It is with this last return and resurrection that we are primarily concerned. Granting the aforesaid premises, it is abundantly apparent that Brahmā-Prajāpati, Puruṣa, Son, First Sacrificer, Cosmic Horse and Tree of Life, in so far as they exist in and of the Three Worlds, could in no way have been thought of as exempt from the universal law of latent causality, *pūrva* or *adṛṣṭa karma.* For the works of Prajāpati, his twin sacrifices (*yajña*), are pre-eminently *kāmya,* desirous: "Prajāpati, desiring offspring (*prajā-kāmya*), sacrificed," *Śatapatha Brāhmaṇa,* II, 4, 4, 1. Prajāpati, in fact, behaves like a Patriarch (*pitṛ*), and as such no other way or voyage can be imagined for him but that of the Patriarchs, the *pitṛyāna*. For deity takes on mortality with all its consequences: hence in the *Bṛhadāraṇyaka Up.*, II, 3, 1, the Brahman in a likeness (*mūrta*) is rightly called mortal, *martya*; his "hundred years" are all of time, but not the timeless.[41] That conception of his mortality is echoed too by Eckhart, "God comes and goes . . . God passes away," "before creatures were, God was not God," "all the Persons being clapt into their nature vanish into the dim silence of their interior being," I, 143, 218, 469; "they become one," *Aitareya Āraṇyaka*, II, 3, 8, "where all existence becometh of one nest," *Mahānârāyaṇa Up.*, II, 3.

Insofar,[42] then, as Deity is in the world, he is bound by Works, his Will or Providence, being however righteous (*dharmya*) comparable to the "ordinary will" based on predilection, is not free: thought of as Ṛtaspati or Dharmarāja, still he is not above the law, not un-just.[43] Free-will, in our sense of the words, represents a contradiction in terms: as the Upaniṣad, cited above, expresses it, and as the Buddhist also felt so strongly, existences are dependent on (*upajīvanti*), the slaves of, their desires, and that holds equally for good and bad desires, for man and for incarnate God. Man's free will consists only in a freedom not to will, a freedom to return to the centre of his being, to identify his own will with His Will who "works willingly but not by will, naturally but not by nature," Eckhart, I, 225. The ordinary will extends only to particular goods; but "the potentiality of the will extends to the universal good . . . just as the object of the intellect extends to universal being," St. Thomas, *Sum. Th.*, I, Q. 105, A. 4: hence, as Nietsche expresses it, "Whoso hath not surrendered will, no will hath he." Free-will is not in the order of nature: he is autonomous (*svarāj*) who knows the Self (*ātman*), but "those whose knowledge is otherwise than this are heteronomous (*anyarājāḥ*), theirs are perishing worlds, in none of all the worlds are they movers-at-will (*kāmacārāḥ*," *Chāndogya Up.*, VII, 25, 2).

If we have seemed to compromise the liberty (*aditiтva*), lordship (*aiśvarya*) or great-Self-hood (*mahâtmya*) of the Person as he is in the world, all the more majestic, more desirable, becomes that Will that is indeed free, his will "whose Will is him-Self," as he is "alone with him-Self," *ēk jō āpai āp*, Kabīr: "self-intent," and "loving only himself," Eckhart.[44] For with the Eye that goes with that Will, he as overseer of *karma*, and we denuded of our virtues, indistinct from and unanimous with Him, are *in posse* to survey the world-picture and to take an infinite delight therein[45]: that picture being his and our eternal play and dalliance, his *līlā*, inhering in him-Self, our-Self—"There has always been this play going on in the Father-nature . . . played eternally before all creatures . . . sport and players are the same," Eckhart, I, 148—"not that this joy first began with the creation, no, for it was from eternity in the great mystery, yet only as a spiritual melody and sport in itself. The creation is the same sport out of himself, viz., a platform or instrument of the Eternal Spirit," Bōhme, *Signatura Rerum*, XVI, 2-3.[46]

Two Trinities (*tridhā*) are mentioned: it is to be understood that both are manifested (*vyakta*) and intelligible (*jñeya*) but the first (Fire, Supernal-Sun, and Spirit) is informal (*arūpa*), the second (the Three Worlds, Earth, Heaven, Firmament) aspectual, (*rūpa*) and perceptible (*dṛśya*). Here the Trinity is called an "arrangement," *dhā*. In the *Taittirīya Up.*, I, 3, 1-4, where five aspects of the fundamental Trinity are explained, the term *saṁhitā*, "grouping" is employed. Eckhart speaks similarly of the Trinity as an "arrangement" and as "articulate speech," the Persons being "illuminations of the understanding."[47]

In our text the body of the aspectual Trinity is conceived in the likeness of a horse. "Meseems that thou art

Varuṇa, O steed . . . speeding with wings on paths fair and dustless," *Ṛg Veda*, I, 163, 4 and 5, and *Taittirīya Saṁhitā*, IV, 6, 7. For Varuṇa was the ancient name of the Supreme Being, Āditya, Supernal-Sun, Child-of-the Liberty. The cosmic horse is more fully described in the first *adhyāya* of our Upaniṣad, corresponding to *Atharva Veda*, X, 7, 32-34. The Sun is his eye, the Wind the breath of his nostrils, Universal Fire his open mouth, the Year his body, stars his bones, clouds his flesh, and he bears angels, choirs, titans and men alike across the nether (*apara*)[48] sea of the possibilities of existence, for the "sea is his kin (*bandhu*), his womb (*yoni*)." In a similar likeness Eckhart speaks of God's delights: "The joy and satisfaction of it are ineffable. It is like a horse turned loose in a lush meadow giving vent to his horse-nature by galloping full-tilt about the field: he enjoys it, and it is his nature. And just in the same way God's joy and satisfaction in his likes finds vent in his pouring out his entire nature and his being into this likeness, for he is this likeness himself," I, 240: compare *Ṛg Veda*, VII, 87, 2, referring to Varuṇa, "The Gale that is thy-Self thunders through the firmament like an untamed stag that takes his pleasure in the fields."

This is a likeness (*mūrti*) and a figure (*pratīka*) connatural with that of the Tree of Life or that of the World-wheel: a figure or image of the Divine Being in extension, space pervading, not forgetting that the locus of this space (*ākāśa*) is in the lotus of the heart. With the becoming of the cosmic horse-body, that of the Three Worlds is established (*pratiṣṭha*) in the Waters. The remainder of the *adhyāya* explains the further becoming of the world in terms of generation and utterance, and with respect to mortality, sacrifice, and regeneration. The horse sacrifice is an imitation[49] of the divine passion and of regeneration: and he who understands, the Comprehensor of this drama, *ya evaṁ vidvān*, has verily performed the sacrifice, and thereby shares in a more abundant life, both here and now in the flesh, and there-beyond in eternity.

He, Death, Privation, willed (*akāmayat*) "Let there be born (*jāyet*) of Me a second Self" (*dvitīya . . . ātman*). By means of the Intellect (*manas*) there came-about a carnal-knowledge (*mithuna*) of the *unspoken*[50] Word (*vāc*). What was the seed (*retas*), that became the Year (*saṁvatsara*). Ere that there was no Year. He let bear him for as long as is the Year, after that poured him forth (*asṛjata*).

When he was born (*jāta*), Death (*mṛtyu*) yawned upon him. He gave out a cry (*bhāṇ*): that became the *spoken*[50] Word (*vāc*). 4.

That is, Godhead already Selfed as Intellect, would go out further into existence. For by and in himself, the Father is an Intellect devoid of intellection, an Energy that does not energise: his paternity is only actualised by the filiation of a Son. The Year, Prajāpati, the Horse, is the begotten Son of God. That is God's understanding of himself, I am *that* I am, the paternal Intellect's conception of the maternal Word; "comprehension belongs to his paternal power," Eckhart, I, 364. "The begotten (*prajā*) is the combination (*sandhi*) of these conjoint principles, begetting (*prajanana* = *maithuna*) the means (*sandhāna*)," *Taittirīya Up.*, I, 3, 3.

That the Year,[51] Brahmā-Prajāpati, the Yakṣa in the Tree of Life, the Cosmic Horse, mortal by nature and immortal in their essence are one and the same as God's only begotten Son incarnate, who died as Jesus but is from Eternity Christ and Logos in the bosom of the Father is à priori apparent from many points of view, for example in the procession by generation, and in the acts of voluntary sacrifice, "himself unto himself." "Who sees Me, sees the Father" may be compared to *Maitri Up.*, VI, 4, and VII, 11, where the One Enlightener (*eka sambodhayitṛ*), the Single Tree (*eka aśvattha*), is called an "everlasting basis for the vision of Brahman." From the standpoint of comparative religion, from His point of view who "left not himself without a witness," *Acts*, XIV, 17, and however distasteful this may be to individual persuasion, the Messiah is One Person.

That the equivalence of the Vedic and Christian Sons of God, of Horse and Lamb for example, is not even more apparent depends primarily on the diversity of scale in the imagery. The Indian embodiment of the only begotten Son is cosmic: human (*pauruṣya*) only ideally as Eternal Man, the single mirror of all existences, not human (*māniṣa*) as a man amongst men. Whereas the Christian Son of God is presented historically precisely in the guise of a man amongst men, born of a woman amongst women, in the fashion of terrestrial *avatāras*, having given names, such as Rāma or Gautama. The same applies to every case in which a religion seems to have been established by a single Founder; for example in Buddhism, where we are given to understand that the man Gautama, Siddhârtha, became Comprehensor (Buddha) at a given time and place. These historical and local points of view are later on transcended: and when it has come to be understood that Christ's birth is eternal, that the enlightenment of the Tathāgata "dates from the beginning of time," then it becomes not merely evident, but can be accepted without anguish, that all alternative-formulations (*paryāya*) are utterances of one and the same Word or Wisdom.

These considerations are of paramount importance for a correct comparative theology. For on the one hand the Year, Brahmā-Prajāpati, is no more and no less a "demiurge" than is Christ-Logos "who causes the whole emanation" and "effects all things," Eckhart, I, 130 and

382[53]: and on the other, the conception of this Christ, this Brahmā as the only begotten is affirmed—" he could never have had but one Son for he is none other than his understanding. Had he a thousand sons they must needs be all the same Son," Eckhart, I, 131, that holds for the Prajāpatis and Buddhas of countless aeons, for Prajāpati, Tammuz, Herakles, Horus, Christ, or " Idea of Muḥammad " in any one aeon. Far too much stress has been laid upon the humanity of Jesus : it were better to remember his perfection.[54] What he took on was not " man," but human nature : the nature not of *vir* but of *homo*, no more masculine than feminine. " Thou art woman, thou art man . . . the seasons and the seas," *Śvetāśvatara Up.*, IV, 3-4 (cf. *Aitareya Āraṇyaka*, II, 3, 8, 5) : " This champion or lion is no man or woman, but he is both," Böhme, *Signatura Rerum*, XI, 43. Far too much stress has been laid upon his birth in Galilee : in reality " there is no time where this birth befalls," " this birth remains in the Father eternally . . . who utters in one single Word the whole of what he knows, the whole of what he can afford, in one single instant, and that instant is eternal." Eckhart, I, 81 and 132 : " It knew, indeed, Itself, viz., that, ' I am Brahman ' ; thereby it became the All," *Bṛhadāraṇyaka Up.*, I, 4, 10. Conceive Him then not as a man but as Universal Man, Person, Fire, or Light : or for easier comparison, as the Lamb of God, for it may be easier to see that sacrificial lamb and sacrificial horse or bull are equivalent illuminations of the understanding. Agnus Dei, Agni Deva.

As for *mithuna*, " progenitive pair," and *maithuna*, " begetting ": generation can only be spoken of with reference to the interaction of conjoint principles, these being here, as also in Christian theology, the Knower and the Known, the Act and the Potentiality of Understanding : " the Holy Ghost was gotten in the Word with this same Intellect," Eckhart, I, 381 and 407, " that by which the Father begets is the divine nature . . . as being that by which the generator generates," St. Thomas, *Sum. Th.*, I, Q. 41, A. 5. Our text takes for granted the second of the conjoint principles, the unuttered Word or Understanding, *vāc*: but we know from other and abundant sources that She is the divine Nature, Prakṛti, Aditi, Virāj, the Waters. She is the silence in Godhead, every possibility and promise of existence, his means whereby, the inexhaustible well of his abundance. But inasmuch as God and Godhead, Heaven and Earth, essence and nature are one in Him, it is an emission of seed not alone on the part of Intellect, pregnancy not only in the Word that has to be understood: it is Deity, not any one of the Persons separately that is pregnant, "He" brings forth.

Retas, "seed," is not only poured forth, but becomes the begotten offspring, and so for example we speak of the "seed of Abraham": compare the account of generation in the *Aitareya Āraṇyaka*, II, 5, and the Self-identity (consubstantiality) of father and son asserted here and elsewhere. The child is "not any new thing, but the very seed of man and woman, and is only bred forth in the mixture, and so only a twig groweth out of the tree," Böhme, *XL Questions concerning the Soule*, VIII, 18. In the *Aitareya Up.*, IV, 1, *retas*, seed, is identified with *tejas*, the Fiery-Energy: elsewhere, e.g., *Mānava Dharmaśāstra* I, 8, *vīrya*, "virility," "virtue," is synonymous. Seed was probably regarded as the vehicle of Spirit, *prâṇa*, for "it is *prâṇa*, verily the Self as pure Intelligence, that grasps and animates the flesh," *Kauṣītaki Up.*, III, 3: that comes very near to the Christian point of view, "the formation of the body taken by the Son is attributed to the Holy Ghost . . . just as the power of the soul which is in the semen, through the spirit enclosed therein, fashions the body in the generation of other men," St. Thomas, *Sum. Th.*, III, Q. 32, A.1.[54a]

Whether the Persons of the Trinity are rightly named: though there is not a "real," but only a possible relationship of Persons in Deity antecedent to procession, *solus ante principium*, all tradition is agreed that the notion of generation, taken from our knowledge of living things, is with respect to the Son analogically appropriate.[55] Consistency then requires diversity of sex in the conjoint principles invoked : as explicitly in our Upaniṣad, I, 5, 7, "The Father is Intellect (*manas*), the Mother Wisdom (*vāc*), the Child Spirit (*prâṇa*)."[56] Wisdom, *vāc*, is rightly feminine in Vedic thought, for She is the divine nature, the Waters antecedent to their counter-shining, *mūla-prakṛti*, dark undifferentiated, passive Godhead : not distinct from the Father in the Unity, but distinguished from him in the eternal act of generation, as the sea is from the sun. So the Mother is the second Person of the Vedic Trinity, as the Son, the Year, Prajāpati, is logically the third. Spirit, *prâṇa*, is not here a distinct Person, but primarily an essential name of the Father ; and in hypostasis, an essential name of the Son. The procession of the Spirit is naturally a spiration (*samīraṇa*) : but when Spirit, Life, becomes an essential name of the Son, then the procession, *ipso facto*, must be called a filiation. In this sense the birth of the Son is a divided act, "I proceeded out of the *mouth* of the Most High, to wit out of the natural *conception* of the essential word of the divine Father," Eckhart, I, 269 : and in Islamic theology, the Idea of Muḥammad is at once the Spirit of Allāh and his son.[57]

Vedic Logos doctrine is better reflected in Greek than in orthodox Christian doctrine.[58] The problem is too complex for full discussion here, but it may be pointed out that Vedic *ṛtam* and *dharman* are "neuter" (*aliṅga*, "without specific gender," but not excluding possibility of gender), and are to be thought of as essential names equivalent to later Brahman and the Imperishable-Word (*akṣaram*) OṀ, also epicene : in other words, the Indian Logos doctrine neither excludes the unity of Essence and Nature, nor their distinction as conjoint principles linked in joint procession by way of generation or utterance.

It will be understood that Vedic "theology" takes account of two distinct Trinities. In the one arrangement (Agni, Āditya, Vāyu; Rudra, Viṣṇu, Brahmā) the Persons are distinguished by their natures (the characteristic *guṇas* being *tamas*, *sattva*, and *rajas*); the names are essential and the relations mutual and reversible, so that any two may be thought of as aspects or emanations of the first, there being no logical order of manifestation. In the other arrangement (Supernal Sun and Waters—or Heaven and Earth—and Agni Vaiśvānara or Āyus; Śiva, Śakti, Kumāra; Manas, Vāc, Prâṇa, etc.), the Persons are distinguished by naturally progenitive relationships, *quâ* Father, Mother, and Offspring, the names take on a more personal character, and there is a logical order of procession. The Christian and Indian Trinities can only be rightly compared when it is realised that while the Christian Father, Son, and Spirit correspond directly to Āditya, Agni Vaiśvānara, and Vāyu (procession being by way of utterance or spiration, not a generation), Father and Son, when the latter is spoken of as begotten by generation from "conjoint principles" (St. Thomas, *Sum. Th.*, I, Q. 27, A. 2), or as "his understanding of himself," correspond also to Manas and Prâṇa, and to Agni and Agni Vaiśvānara ("born of the Waters" or "born of Earth," and whose nature is exemplary). There is lacking, then, in the Christian formulation, when the Son is thought of as natural and begotten, that Person who should be the second of the "conjoint principles," which principles can be no other than his Essence and his Nature; no "Wisdom" or "Nature," corresponding to Vāc or Prakṛti, is recognized as a Person in the Christian arrangement of God. It is true that Christ takes on fleshly nature from—"is natured by"—the Virgin Mary, and that she is therefore called the "Mother of God," but that is not with respect to his eternal procession, merely with respect to the accident of his birth in Galilee. Abstracted from eventful generation, Christ is motherless.

It is only in effect and tacitly, if not under protest, that with the Assumption and Coronation of the Virgin, and Mariolatry generally, that Mother Nature, Wisdom, *natura naturans*, Prakṛti, Vāc, Māyā, is restored to her numinous bridal throne.

That is made explicit when Eckhart says that "it is God who has the treasure and the bride in him," I, 381, "the Godhead wantons with the Word, I, 388, "from the Father's embrace of his own nature comes the eternal playing of the Son," I, 148, "where personal understanding keeps to its unity of nature and has intercourse therewith, there the Father-nature has maternal names and is doing mother's work, for it is exclusively mother's work to receive the seed of the eternal Word," and in the divine light "stood Mary always, bearing her divine child," I, 404, as naturally follows if we take it that Christ's birth is eternal.[59] Nothing here contradicts that the Spirit is the common spiration, common love and mutual regard of the Three Persons.

With our Upaniṣad, I, 1, 2, *tasya samudre yoniḥ,* "in the sea is his womb," may be compared St. Augustine, *Sermonae*, 124, *processit . . . de utero virginali*; Eckhart's "in the bare chamber of the virgin heart of their chosen vessel Mary . . . out of chaos a shining spiritual soul emerged," I, 463, 464; and Petrarch, *Vergine bella, che di sol vestita, coronata di stelle, al sommo sole piacesti si che'n te sua luce ascose,* ". . . to the Supernal Sun thou didst seem so fair, that in thee he hid his Light," a noteworthy parallel to the many Vedic passages in which the Angels are represented as seeking for the hidden Sun or Fire, and finding him reflected or brought to birth in the Waters. Dante, "Virgin Mother, daughter of thy Son . . . fixed goal of the eternal counsel . . . in thy womb was lit again the love under whose heat in the eternal peace this flower unfolded," *Paradiso*, XXXIII. A "Tantrik" ideology of this kind is characteristically developed in the gnostic conception of Sophia as a primordial Aeon, and especially in Valentinian gnosticism, where the Propater Bythos has for his "śakti" Ennoia, "Thought," or Sige, "Silence," from whom are begotten Nous and Aletheia as first principles of manifestation. Finally, it may be observed that in the systematic language of the *Bṛhad Devatā* and *Nirukta*, the Father would be called a celestial, the Mother a chthonic, and the Son an aerial divinity.

"For as long as is the year": that long time would be the same as the "night" of the deep sleep of Brahman, as distinguished from the following "day" or "year" of the Brahman's waking, during which the horse runs free, as explained in the seventh stanza. Cf. *Mānava Dharmaśāstra*, I, 12, *tasminaṇḍe sa bhagavânuṣitvā parivatsaram.*

"The Year is Prajāpati," *Maitri Up.*, I, 5, 14: "the Year, verily, is Prajāpati, is Time (*kāla*),[60] the nesting-place (*nīḍa*) of Brahman, Self . . . this formal Time is the great ocean of begotten existences (*prajā*) . . . this whole universe here, and whatsoever of weal or woe may be seen therein . . . he who offers and likewise he who receives the offerings . . . Viṣṇu, Prajāpati," *Maitri Up.*, VI, 15-16, "for the Brahman has two forms, Time (*kāla*) and the Timeless (*akāla*)," *ibid.*

That is, while the Son "remains within as essence and goes forth as Person . . . things flowed forth finite into time while abiding infinite in eternity . . . in this image, everything is God; sour and sweet, good and bad, all are one in this image," Eckhart, I, 271, 285, 286.

"Death yawned upon him,"[61] that is upon the new-born Year, now God has taken on mortality, *nirṛtim ā viveśa*, *Ṛg Veda*, I, 164, 32: existence, life, is a modality of being naturally subject to mortality, "sure is death for the born, sure is birth for the dead," *Bhagavad Gītā*, II, 27, cf. the vision of Deity there as all-devouring Time, Ch. XI.

"He gave out a cry": viz., "the hidden name whereby

thou didst beget all that is and shall be," *Ṛg Veda*, X, 55, 2, wording (*vāc*) is indeed his Word (*vāc*), *Bṛhadāraṇyaka Up.*, I, 1, 1. Cf. *Ṛg Veda*, I, 163, 1, "Thy great birth from the Pleroma (*purīṣa*) and from the sea (*samudra*), O Steed, is to be magnified, in that thou didst neigh (*akranda*) when first born, whose are the wings of the falcon and the limbs of the deer"; and *Taittirīya Saṁhitā*, IV, 2, 8, "When first thou didst cry on birth, arising from the sea, the foam, that is thy famed birth, O Steed." "In the beginning this (universe) was unuttered (*avyāhṛta*)" *Maitri Up.*, VI, 6; but by that utterance (*vyāhṛti*) of Prajāpati's, in which all things are called by their essential names,[62] their existence was poured forth (*asṛgram*),[63] "for all these existences are Principles (*manas*, "Intellect"),[64] *Pañcaviṁśa Brāhmaṇa*, VI, 9, 14, 20. "One should know that all these verses (*ṛc*), all these Vedas, all sounds, are merely one Utterance (*vyāhṛti*), verily Spiration (*prāṇa*), Spiration verily the verses," *Aitareya Āraṇyaka*, II, 2, 2. Just as in Christianity, "God spake never a word but one," Eckhart, I, 148, "in this only Word he spoke all things," I, 377, for "the Word of the Father is his understanding of himself," I, 146, "the Father spoke himself and all creatures in the Word . . . to all creatures in his Son," I, 377, or again "First out of the Father there leaps forth the Son, small but so puissant in his Godly strength that it is he who causes the whole emanation. The second sally is the premier angel, following hard upon the first event. It speeds apace . . . so charged with power that given a thousand or more worlds they would be wanting in capacity ere the first issue had been spent. . . . One unique throw with the world a sheet of water and the water would fail ere the circles died away," Eckhart, I, 130.

He, *Death*, bethought himself, "Verily, if I shall intend against him, I shall make the less food for myself." With that Word, by that Self, he poured forth (*asṛjata*) all This, whatsoever: the Ṛg, the Yajur, and the Sāma Vedas, metres, sacrifice, men and beasts.

Whatsoever he poured forth, that he began to eat (*ad*). Verily he devours (*ad*) everything: that is the Liberty (*adititva*) of Aditi. He who knows thus the Liberty of Aditi becomes an eater of all things here, everything becomes his food (*anna*). 5.

The first part continues the thought of the preceding stanza, and needs little explanation. "The less food," i.e., the less life. "With that Word, by that Self," viz., from the mouth of the Year, Prajāpati, and here we must understand a neighing of the Horse.

"That he began to eat": that is Death, Godhead, began to live, to exist as God: as we have already seen, God's existent being depends on his existent world no less than its existent being depends on him, each presupposes the other. Not in causal relation, but in reciprocity and simultaneity, here there "is no distinction save outpouring and outpoured . . . they are one God . . . begetter and suddenly begotten," Eckhart, I, 72.

It is that same fiery mouth that utters all existences, and whereunto they hasten back; in our Upaniṣad, I, 1, 1, "Universal Fire his open mouth,"[65] cf. *Maitri Up.*, VI, 2, "all-devouring Time," *Bhagavad Gītā*, XI, 32, *kālo'smi . . . lokānsamāhartum iha pravṛttaḥ*, "I am come-forth as Time, for the destruction of the worlds," and *Ṛg Veda*, I, 164, 44, "one of these (Agni) mows down at the end of the year."

As for the "Liberty," *adititva*, of Aditi: this is the fundamental meaning of the name Aditi, the ancient Mother-goddess, the supreme feminine power in the Vedas (e.g., *Ṛg Veda*, I, 89, 10), second Person of the Trinity, Mahādevī and Śakti of later texts. Aditi is the mother-mate of Varuṇa, who as sprung from Her, though not by generation, is pre-eminently Āditya, Child of the Infinite, and Supernal-Sun: Mother-Nature, the same as Virāj, "Sovran-Light," from whom all things "milk" their specific virtues and proper operation, *Atharva Veda*, VII, 1, VIII, 9-10, and IX, 1: *Vāc*, the means of utterance: *Āpaḥ*, the Waters, all the possibilities of existence, un-limited (*a-diti*) by particular conditionings·*Mahāmāyā*, Bōhme's Magic, "a mother in all three worlds, and makes each thing after the model of that thing's will . . . a creatrix according to the understanding, and lends itself to good or to evil . . . ground and support of all things," *Sex Puncta Mystica*, V, 11 and 20: "Tao," as the "Mother of all things," *Tao Tê Ching*, I, 1. "Contained in the Father as nature . . . *wherefore* he is omnipotent . . . for the Godhead has all things *in posse* . . . (and) flows into creatures. It gives to each as much as it can hold; to stones their existence, to the trees their growth, to birds their flight, to beasts their pleasures, to the angels reason (? *sc.* intellect), to man free nature (*sc.* free will)," Eckhart, I, 371-372: that is, to every existence its own virtue and idiosyncrasy.

So then, *nirguṇa* Brahman, *amūrta* Brahman, are the same as Aditi, Virāj, the Waters; and the *Bhagavad Gītā* is in complete accord with Vedic tradition when it declares "My womb (*yoni*) is the Great (*mahat* = *para* = *nirguṇa*) Brahman; in it I bestow the germ (*garbha*), thence cometh the becoming (*saṁbhava*) of all existences," XIV, 3: and further, when Kṛṣṇa, after listing the material elements of existence, adds, "That is my empirical (*apara*) Nature (*prakṛti*). Know thou my transcendental (*para*) Nature (*prakṛti*) as another (*anya*), as the elements of life (*jīva*-) whereby the universe is held-in-being (*dhārayate*), know this to be the womb (*yoni*) of all existences," VII, 5 and 6. Just as in *Bṛhadāraṇyaka Up.*, I, 1, 2, we find *samudro yoni*, corresponding to *Muṇḍaka Up.*, III, 1, 3, *brahma-yoni*, respectively "whose womb is the sea," and " whose womb is (*para-*) Brahman." Kṛṣṇa's exposition of his two " natures " is perfectly " correct " (*pramiti*).[66] *Para* and *apara prakṛti* are the same as the Upper (*parastāt*) and the Nether (*avastāt*) Waters of *Ṛg Veda*, III, 22, 3, etc. ; as the " two seas " of Varuṇa,[67] which are his " paunches " or " wombs," *udara, kukṣi*,[68] *Atharva Veda*, IV, 16, 3 ; as the " twin breasts " of Aditi, Mother and Honey-whip, that " milk out refreshment," life, *ibid.*, IX, 1, 7.

He willed, " Let me offer up again by a further sacrifice " (*yajña*). He strove, he undertook intension. When he had striven and was intensified, his glorious virility (*yaśovīrya*) went-forth (*udakrāmat*). So when the life-breaths had gone forth (*prâṇeṣu utkrānteṣu*), the body (*śarīra*) began to swell (*śva*). Yet the Intellect (*manas*) remained in the body.[68a] 6.

He, that is the Year, Prajāpati, the Son. A " further sacrifice " implies a former sacrifice : that was the first procession or flowing out into existence, the taking on of personal (*pauruṣya*) nature, and mortality. For all utterance is an incontinence : to " spend " is to " die," and in taking on existence, God takes on mortality : that is the Fisher King's " debility," the meaning of the Grail " myth."

Utkram is used of " going forth," much as in our colloquial " passing out." Either with respect to natural death, whether voluntary and sacrificial as here in our text, or involuntary as in our Upaniṣad, III, 2, 11-12, and *Kauṣītaki Up.*, I, 2, 12-15[69] : or in connection with *avataraṇa*, the " appearance on the stage of life " of an *avatāra*, which is at once a descent[70] from heaven to earth and a death in heaven, " His exit thence is his entrance here," Eckhart, I, 132, "Falling into time, they droop and fade," *ibid.*, 244. The technical equivalent of (*ut-*) *krama* (= *kramôdaya*, *prasaraṇa*) is "procession," with respect to *avataraṇa*: as when *tejas*, the Fiery-Energy, proceeds (*utkramya*) in the Tree of Life, as it branches forth into space, *Maitri Up.*, VII, 11, or when the Great Yakṣa resting on the back of the Waters is described as "by intension proceeding" (*tapasi krānta*) in the world-tree, *Atharva Veda*, X, 7, 38. That going out, that incarnation of the Year, Prajāpati, was the "first sacrifice."

Now having taken on flesh in the bodily form of the Cosmic horse or World Tree, incarnate deity would save from its incurred mortality that body which is the sum of all existences. He suffers therefore a Passion, viz., intension and death, that is the "further sacrifice"; as emphasized in the concluding verse, "he sacrificed himself to himself," and *Ṛg Veda*, X, 90, 15, where the "Angels" (Persons of the Trinity), acting as sacrificial priests, "sacrificed with the sacrifice unto the Sacrifice." That concept of self-sacrifice and voluntary passion, undertaken or suffered to the end that life may be made more abundant recurs throughout the Vedas and in the traditions of many peoples. Here we need allude only to the Christian parallel, the Crucifixion on the Tree of Life: for the Cross, the Rood, is a "tree," the Tree of Life, its trunk the axle-tree of being, its arms or branches all extension on every plane of being, "the gift of God is the positive existence of all creatures in the Person of his Son," Eckhart, I, 427. The identity of Cross and Tree is too familiar to need particular demonstration here,[71] nevertheless the phraseology of Böhme, *Signatura Rerum*, XIV, 32, may be remarked, "Now the flash, when it is enkindled by the liberty, and by the cold fire, makes in its rising a cross with the comprehension of all properties; for here arises the spirit in the essence, and it stands thus: If thou hast here understanding, thou needest ask no more; it is eternity and time, God in love and anger, moreover heaven and hell." Equally consonant with the thought of the Vedas and Upaniṣads are Swinburne's moving lines :

> " The tree many rooted
> That swells to the sky
> With frondage red-fruited
> The life-tree am I . . .
> In me only the root is
> That blooms in your boughs . . .
> My own blood is what stanches
> The wounds in my bark. . . ."

The efficacy of the ritual sacrifice (*karma, yajña*), that the ritual undertaken with a given end in view assuredly procures that end, is by no means denied in the Upaniṣads. The end in view, however, is a renewal and magnification of life, not an absolute emancipation from mortality. Knowledge alone, That *art* thou, is the realisation of immortality, in or regardless of any here or now. So then there is a higher sacrifice, his who understands, *ya evaṁ veda*, the ritual not only in its imitative operation here, as a thing per-formed,[72] but in its intrinsic-form as a thing un-formed, re-turned, there in the uttermost Empyrean, the lotus of the heart. And that applies not only to specific rituals, such as the horse-sacrifice or offering of *soma*, but to all the functions of life, which if they are undertaken blindly and desirously increase the sum of our mortality, but if undertaken undesirously, and unselfishly but Self-ishly, and with an understanding of their spiritual, transubstantial equivalents, are by no means obstacles, but rather ways of enlightenment. What is here involved is transformation (*parāvṛtti, abhisambhava*),[73] or in terms of psychology, sublimation : in religious extension, " Except a man be born again." All that is further developed in the *Bhagavad Gītā*, e.g., IV, 27, 32 and 33, " Others pour out as their sacrifice all the functioning of the senses (*indriya-*

karmāṇi) and all those of life (*prâṇa-karmāṇi*) in the fire of the discipline of self-restraint (*ātmasaṁyogâgnau*) which is lit by wisdom (*jñāna-dīpite*) . . . many and various are the sacrifices thus outspread before the face of God (Brahman), but all these are by way of works, which if thou understand is thy release ; better than the sacrifice of any objects is that of wisdom, therewith are works undone in gnosis (*jñāne parisamāpyate*), naught remaining over."

Returning more directly to our text, what was the body of the horse suffers corruption and " swells up,"[74] it is no longer a living horse, but de-natured, its horsiness (*aśvatta*) has gone out of it. The flesh becomes " food " and life for other existences, as before explained. Intellect, the Principle of existence, Self-same in the Father and the Son, only remains incarnate, though in another nature and other individual existences or permutations (*pariṇāma*) : for That " is indestructible, perpetual, unborn, undiminished, not slain when the body is slain," *Bhagavad Gītā*, II, 20 and 21. So, just as we saw previously that the living universe had no " first " beginning, so now it is asserted in another way that the universe is without end, *sicut erat in principio, et nunc et semper, in saecula saeculorum.*

He willed, " May this my *body* be renewed (*medhya*), may I thereby be Selfed (*ātmanvī*) again. Therewith there-became-again (*samabhavat*) a horse (*aśva*). " That horse (*aśva*) has-been-made-whole (*medhyam-abhūd*), he thought (*iti*). That is verily the horse-whole-nature (*aśvamedhatva*) of the horse-sacrifice (*aśvamedha*). He knows indeed the Aśvamedha, who knows it thus.

He beheld him intellectually (*tam . . . manyata*), not restraining him. After as long as is a year, he sacrificed him to him-Self. *Other sacrificial* beasts (*paśu*) he delivered over to the Angels. Therefore they sacrifice the victim dedicated to Prajāpati as though to the Several Angels (*sarva daivatya*).

The Sacrifice-that-is-the-horse (*aśvamedha*) is verily he who intensifies (*tapati*) : it-Self is the Year, Prajāpati. This *sacrificial* fire is the Sheen (*arka*) : the *Three* Worlds (*lokāḥ*) are its Hypostases (*ātmānaḥ*).

Twain are these, the Sheen and the Sacrifice-that-is-the-Horse (*aśvamedha*). Yet again they are One Angel, even Death (*mṛtyu*). He who knows this, forfends mortality (*punar mṛtyu*), death (*mṛtyu*) gets him not, Death (*mṛtyu*) becomes him-Self, of these Angels he becomes the Unity.

This last section of the *adhyāya* describes the resurrection of the Horse, the perpetuation of life. Here the meaning of *medhya* is of primary importance. The word *medhya* is commonly rendered " sacrificial," " fit for sacrifice," but these meanings are secondary to the primary sense of " fit," " strong," " vigorous," " whole," " virile," " free from blemish." These primary meanings are the valid ones in our context, for the sacrifice has been made already, and now life is renewed : there is a resurrection and rebecoming of the horse, a new, re-newed, horse-nature, horsiness has been made whole again.

" Beheld him intellectually," that is " remembered " him " for as long as is a year " : that means kept him, these Three Worlds, in living being throughout the cycle of angelic time, the life-time of a Brahmā-Prajāpati, that is a " day " of supernal time, during which the Brahman " wakes." His remembrance is our existence.[75] But as the soul " honours God most in being quit of God," " it remains for her to be somewhat that he is not," it is "God's full intention" that she should "relinquish her existence," that "means the death of the spirit,"[76] so in "strange words she prays "Lord, my welfare lies in thy never calling me to mind," Eckhart, I, 274 and 376. That point of view is implicit in the conclusion of the *adhyāya*, where the Comprehensor forfends mortality, becomes im-mortal in full identity (*sāyujya*) with Death. Immortality is not eternal life, but a never being born, for only what is never born can never die: Death-absolute transcends existence and non-existence, *sat* and *asat* at once, all good and evil. In the meantime, existence is the primary good, the *raison d'être* of the sacrifice, "nothing can *wish* it did not exist," *He* cannot in Person will the non-existence of his worlds before the end of time, "these worlds would be destroyed did I not work works," *Bhagavad Gītā*, III, 24, who willed that he might have possessions to the end that he might "work works," *Bṛhadāraṇyaka Up.*, I, 4, 17. Note that to "work works," *karmāṇi kṛ*, is also a technical expression equivalent to "to perform sacrifices," "celebrate offices."

"Not restraining him": that is, permitting the cycle of existence, our "process of evolution," to run its course without interference, subject only to the natural consequentiality of accidents, the latent (*apūrva*) and unforeseen (*adṛṣṭa*) working of past events. As we have already seen, what He bestows is life (*prāṇa*), not mode or species: "He emanates neither agency nor acts," *na kartatvanna karmāṇi sṛjati*, it is the proper-nature of each thing that operates," *svabhāvastu pravartate, Bhagavad Gītā*, V, 14, "what should restraint effect?" *nigrahaḥ kiṁ kariṣyati, ibid.*, III, 33, Wisdom lies in the knowledge that it is not "I," not "Self" that acts, "'I do not anything' should he think who is a bridled-man[77] and knows the suchness," *naiva kiṁcitkaromîti yukto manyet tattvavid, ibid.*, V, 8, thus acting unattached, Eckhart's "willingly but not from will," he is liberated-from-the-pairs (*nirdvandvaḥ*) loosed from bondage (*bandhāt pramucyate*), V, 30, attaining, in the terms of our text, the Liberty (*adititva*) of Aditi.

So then at the end of the " year," cosmic or terrestrial as the case may be, the horse is sacrificed, its life-breaths returning to him whose image it is, not as he is in hypostasis (*dvitīya ātman*), but in the Unity, there " the Son is lost in the unity of the essence," Eckhart, I, 275. Just as all " souls " (*bhūtāni*) are returned into His universal nature at the end of time, *Bhagavad Gītā*, IX, 8, so the " soul " of the horse is returned to its source when it is ritually slain: that is done with an end in view, that life may be renewed, just as at the beginning of time, of any time, in the spring of the " year," all " souls " are poured forth again from their latency in him, *ibid.*

The cosmic Aśvamedha is the willed Passion of incarnate deity, begotten Second Person (*dvitīya ātman*), this his further sacrifice being a denial of the will to life, as the first was its assertion. But this Passion and formally undertaken death are not without an end in view, this also is a desirous work, *kāmya karma*, and as such will have its consequences in a renewed manifestation of life, in another Time, when another Sun, another Horse, will be poured out (*visṛṣṭi*). The terrestrial Aśvamedha is the solemn enactment of that Passion, to the analogous end that life may be renewed, made viable, enhanced and continued here and now, " I ask the seed of the male horse." He who undertakes the rite accordingly, with an eye to its fruits, wins fullness of life on earth (a hundred years, in the analogy of His " hundred years "), wealth, offspring, cattle, whatever he desires here, and therewith also the world of the Patriarchs, after his death: that is not a final emancipation, for the natural reward of interested works is inevitable, he must return again to renewed birth, *punar apādana*, and other deaths, *punar mṛtyu*. He only who knows, who understands, who realises and so performs the rite intellectually, who knows Self-evidently that the horse is transubstantially Prajāpati, the Year, the Son, wins either now or in due course, according to the perfection of his realisation, back to Intellect, to Brahman, and is thus delivered, he only forfends mortality, being one with Death, in and of the Supreme Identity, One Angel.

"Forfends immortality," then what? That is, in the last analysis beyond our ken, which can extend only to the operation of the Persons, that is beyond the ken of God himself as Person, "he knows or knows not," as the *Ṛg Veda*, X, 129, 7, expresses it. For the thing known being in the knower always and only according to the mode of the knower, existence can know only of existence. He only *is*, without a second whom he might know, or by whom He might be known. So then he only "who knows 'I am Brahman' becomes this All . . . whoever worships any other Angel than him-Self, thinking 'He is one and I another,' he knows not, he can only be likened to a sacrificial animal fit to be offered to the Angels," *Bṛhadāraṇyaka Up.*, I, 4, 10.[78]

What lies there beyond the order of nature, on the farther shore of time, is compared by the Veda either to dreamless sleep, or to a fourth state of simultaneous sleep and waking; that corresponds in Christian phraseology to the "idleness" or "silence," and to the simultaneity of "eternal rest and eternal work." None of this is intelligible to the reason, being inexpressible in terms of thesis and antithesis. Let us see nevertheless what Vedic and Christian seers have told of that primordial and modeless state of being.

It is implied in the doctrine of reflection, that the Self is present in the world throughout time, and that the world-picture and all therein is similarly present to the Self throughout time, "He, Varuṇa, numbers the winkings of the eyes of men," *Atharva Veda*, IV, 16, 4, "not a sparrow falls to the ground without thy Father's knowledge." What this involves for the individual is very clearly explained in our Upaniṣad, III, 2, 12, where it is said that when a man dies, " what does not go out of him is the name (*nāma*, " noumenon "), that is without-end (*ananta*), and inasmuch as what-is-without-end is the Several Angels, thereby he wins accordingly the world without-end." The Several Angels is the Trinity of Persons, as explained below, p. 64. The notion of " name " has to be understood in connection with that doctrine of the Word, *vāc*, and that of the utterance, *vyāhṛti*, of the worlds : " name " is " idea," and what is meant by the endlessness of names in their persistence as prototypes of acts[79] in the consciousness that is the Self, whose remembrance (*manana*) is our existence (*sthiti*). That is a persistence, as it were of " art in the artist " (Eckhart, 1,285), in the Triune Intellect, or Buddhist Ālaya-vijñāna, what Eckhart calls our " storehouse of ideas and incorporeal forms," I, 402, " God's art," I, 461, " all creatures in their natural mode are exemplified in the divine essence," I, 253. That eternity of individual prototypes of all the accidents of being is by no means the same thing as an individual immortality of the soul, as now conceived, in no way a reward, but purely abstract and " nominal." That is brought out very clearly in the *Kauṣītaki Up.*, II, 12-15, where the immortality of the angelic powers of the soul is not with respect to their specific integration as a given individual, but with respect to the return of the several powers or elements of consciousness to their single source in the knowing Self, almost literally in the words of Eckhart " combining with each divine power she is that power in God," I, 380. That loss of creaturehood, and therewith loss of God as an external object of devotion Eckhart calls the " lowest death of the soul on her way to divinity," I, 274.

We do not mean to say that a perpetuity (*sthayitā*) of individual consciousness without further change of state during part or all of time, and corresponding more nearly to the popular idea of immortality, is excluded from the possibilities of existence. On the contrary, such perpetuities are envisaged as attainable by those who are not yet Comprehensors, but are in the way to understand, or have acquired merit by good works. Such a perpetuity is on one or another of the lower planes of angelic existence, where the angels-by-works enjoy the fruits of works. Here at the best she reaches the Empyrean heaven, and finds herself in her eternal prototype, her " name " written in the Book of Life, herself as she is in the manifested Son. There " when the soul puts off her creature nature there flashes out its uncreated prototype (= *nāma*) wherein the soul discovers herself in uncreatedness . . . according to the property of the image," Eckhart, I. 275. That is, she finds herself in the exemplar, Christ, Lamb, Horse, Prajāpati, the Year, in her " potential, her essential, intellectual nature . . . revealed in its perfection, in its flower, where it first burgeons forth in the ground of its existence, and all conceived where God conceives himself—that is happiness," Eckhart, I, 290 and 82. There being " one with God in operation " (*pravartana*), " creatures are her subjects, all submitting to her as though they were her handiwork," Eckhart, I, 290. " There perfect, ripe, and whole is each desire ; in it alone is every part, there where it ever was, for it is not in space nor hath it poles," Dante, *Paradiso*, XXII, 64-67. There the will, being well-nigh naughted, is well-nigh free ; for as Boethius expresses it, " the nearer a thing is to the First Mind, the less it is involved in the chain of fate " ; that is, the nearer any consciousness may be to the centre of the gyroscope of causal becoming, *saṁsāra*, *bhava-cakra*,[80] the less is consciousness determined or constrained by external necessity, the more autonomous.

But however glorious, however desirable such an estate may be, whatever bliss beyond imagination

(*Bṛhadāraṇyaka Up.*, IV, 3, 33, *Taittirīya Up.*, II, 8), as "this is not the summit of divine union so it is not the soul's abiding place," Eckhart, I, 276, cf. 410, "that is a resting place (*viśrāma*), not a re-turn (*nivṛti*)," actually "there is no extinction (*nirvāṇa*) without omniscience (*sarvajña*)," *Saddharma Puṇḍarīka*, V, 74, 75, "not till she knows all that there is to be known does she cross over to the unknown good," Eckhart, I, 385. So this is neither from the Indian nor the Christian point of view a final end. For that "eternal nature wherein the soul now finds herself in her exemplar is characterised by multiplicity—the Persons being in separation. . . . Now Christ says: 'No man cometh to the Father but through me.' . . . Though the soul's abiding place is not in him yet she must, as he says, go through him. This breaking through is the second death of the soul and is far more momentous than the first," Eckhart, I, 275: "he invites us to enter by the door of his emanation and return into the source whence we came forth . . . the gate through which all things return perfectly free to their supreme felicity," Eckhart, I, 400. That answers to the Vedic image of the Supernal-Sun, Āditya, as the gateway-of-the-worlds (*loka-dvāra*), whereby there is an entrance (*prapadana*) for the Comprehensor into Paradise (*prâṇârāma*, playground of the Spirit) but which is a barrier (*nirodha*) to the foolish (*avid*), *Chāndogya Up.*, VIII, 6, 6[81]: "there is no approach by a side path here in the world," *Maitri Up.*, VI, 30; "Puruṣa, of the cast(e) of the Sun . . . only by knowing Him does one pass over death," *Śvetāśvatara Up.*, III, 8. It is also as the Supernal-Sun that Viṣṇu is called the "door-keeper" of the Angels, and opens for the understanding sacrificer this door, *Aitareya Brāhmaṇa*, I, 36. That "Agni arose aloft, touching the sky: he opened the door of the world of heaven, verily Agni is the overlord of the world of heaven," *ibid.*, III, 42, corresponds to the "myth" of Christ's ascension and being seated in condominium at the right hand of the Father. Kristos and Agni, Son of God, and Sacrifice reflected on the Supernal-Sun, are that one Angel with the Flaming Sword who guards the gates of Paradise, and one Way-leader on the narrow path that leads across the Upper and the Nether Waters to the Grail Kingdom. There proven by degrees, perfected (*sukṛta*) man, emancipated from individual modality, takes his seat at last with Brahman on "the seat 'Far shining' . . . which is 'Wisdom' (*prajñā*) . . . and the throne 'Unmeasured Life' . . . and to him Brahman says, 'The Waters verily are my world, and are thine,'" *Kauṣītaki Up.*, I, 3-7. So he comes into Lordship (*aiśvarya*) over all the possibilities of existence.

But that Plenum (*pūrṇa*), that Wisdom (*prajñā*), that Self (*ātman*), and Spirit (*prāṇa*) are not the end.[82] There remains for the soul thus lost in and one with (*sāyujya*) the Father a last death, *parimara*, *parinirvāṇa*, *fanā al-fanā*, the "Drowning" and "Despiration": there where "God himself gives up the ghost . . . abiding to himself unknown, in agnosia and a-perception" she must give up her-Self and God him-Self in a naughting of their common "name" and coincident intrinsic "aspect," there she must abandon "name and aspect," however ideally conceived. . . . "Everything must go. The soul must subsist in absolute nothingness. . . . The third nature out of which the soul goes is the exuberant divine nature energising in the Father . . . the soul has got to die to all the activity denoted by the divine nature if she is to enter the divine essence where God is altogether idle.[83] This supernal image is the paradigm whereto the soul is brought by her (last) dying . . . dead and buried in the Godhead and the Godhead lives for none other than itself,"[84] Eckhart, I, 274-278: so also Blake, "I will go down to self-annihilation and Eternal Death, lest the Last Judgment come and find me unannihilate, and I be seiz'd and giv'n into the hands of my own Self-hood."

Those are sayings no more comfortable than the hardest to be found in Indian scripture, and correspond to what is said when our Upaniṣad speaks of Death as the last end and meaning of our life, or when the Śūnyavādin exhausts the categories of negation in defining man's true goal. That is the Liberty of the In-finite, *aditer-adititva*, *Bṛhadāraṇyaka Up.*, I, 2, 5, " free as the Godhead in its non-existence," Eckhart, I, 382: " When I go back into the ground, into the depths, into the well-spring of the Godhead, no one will ask me whence I came or whither I went," I, 143.

This end is hidden " in the darkness of the everlasting Godhead, and is unknown, and never was known, and never will be known," Eckhart,[85] being in its nature and by definition unknowable. There Self—our-Self, him-Self—both sleeps and wakes, sees and sees not, at once fontal and inflowing, modeless and modi-fied, that is all one and the same to the Supreme Indiscrimination. Though we speak of that sleeping and that waking as nights and days of supernal time, that night and day, darkness and sunshine, are not like ours in succession, but simultaneous. For there there is no distinction of unknown potentiality and conscious act: and that is precisely *what*, Vedic *ka*, we cannot understand, who proceed from potentiality to act, and think of " being " only in terms of consciousness.

That *what* we cannot understand is not therefore remote from us, " Heaven is at all points equidistant from the earth," Eckhart, I, 172; nearest and dearest, nesting in the lotus of the heart, inaccessible to knowledge, *That art thou*. Whether we think of That as Selfed and form-ed in Person, or of the Person as therein Self-less, name-less, form-less, it is all One Angel, One transcending knowing and unknowing, gnosis and agnosia. It is just " as these flowing rivers that tend toward the sea, their name and aspect are shattered, it is only spoken of as ' Sea ' " *Praśna Up.*, VI, 5: " as the drop becomes the ocean . . . so the soul imbibing God turns into God," Eckhart, I, 242. In the words of Ruysbroeck,[86] "traversing all worlds of being . . . the rivers pour ceaselessly into this ocean . . . whence there is no return . . . an abyss of darkness, fathomless, limitless, and without qualities, above the names of created things, above the names of God . . . nameless, yet the central point where all names are one. It is the mountain crest of human effort and the abyss of transcendent essence": that is ". . . nostre pace, à qual mare, al qual tutto si move . . .", Dante, *Paradiso*, III, 85-86.

"His, verily, is that (true) aspect of his which is beyond desires, free from ill, without fear. As a man locked in the embrace of a darling bride, knows naught of a within nor a without, so the Person, embraced by Wisdom, by the Self, knows naught of a within nor a without . . . his desire is satisfied, him-Self is his Will (*kāma*), without Will (*akāma*), without care. . . . There the father becomes not a father; a mother not a mother; the angels not the angels; the Vedas not Veda; a thief not a thief . . . he is not followed after by merit, nor followed by demerit, for he has crossed beyond all anguish of the heart . . . he sees though he does not see . . . tastes though he does not taste, speaks though he does not speak, touches though he touches not," *Bṛhadāraṇyaka Up.*, IV, 3, 21-29[87]: "there," as Eckhart, I, 360, quotes from the "Book of Love," "there heard I without sound, there saw I without light, there breathed I without motion, there did I taste what savoured not, there did I touch what touched not back. Then my heart was bottomless, my soul loveless, my mind formless, and my nature natureless." There where Void shines into Void, Deep answers unto Deep, unattainable by thought but all-contained in the lotus of the heart, there is the Supreme Identity, the source and end of life, One Angel, even Death, the Father of Life.

Whispers of heavenly death murmur'd I hear . . .
Darest thou now O soul,
Walk out with me toward the unknown region,
Where neither ground is for the feet nor any path
to follow ?

All waits undreamed of in that region, that inaccessible land.

II

PORTIONS OF THE MAITRI UPANIṢAD

The following translation of parts of the *Maitri Upaniṣad*, describing the procession of the Tree of Life, as a Burning Bush, is offered without comment :

Sixth Prapāṭhaka, 1-4

He bears himself twofold : as the Spirit here, (*prâṇa*) and yonder as the Supernal-Sun (*āditya*).[88] Likewise, indeed, are twain these paths of his, an inner and an outer ; and their revolution is accomplished with the day and night. Yonder Supernal-Sun is verily the outer-Self, the Spirit is the inner-Self. Hence, the motion of the inner-Self is to be measured by that of the outer Self. For thus has it been said : " Whosoever is a Comprehensor, freed from guilt, an over-seer of the senses, of washed-white intellect, whose looking is within, is even He." *And conversely*, the motion of the outer-Self is to be measured by that of the inner-Self. For thus has it been said : " Lo, that Golden Person who is within the Supernal-Sun, and who from his golden station looks down upon this *earth*, is even He who dwells consuming food in the Lotus of the Heart.[88a]

He who dwells existent in the Lotus of the

Heart, consuming food, is that same numinous Solar Fire that is spoken of as all-consuming Time.

What is the Lotus and of what modality (*-maya*)? This Lotus is verily the same as Space.[89] These four airts and inter-airts are its surrounding petals.

These twain, the Spirit and the Supernal-Sun go forth towards each other. One should laud them with that Imperishable-Word OṀ, with the Utterances, *Bhūr, Bhuvas, Svar,* and with the Sāvitrī, " *That Fiery-Energy of Savitṛ, be ours the vision of that Angel's glory, may He incite our Understanding.*"[90]

There are verily two forms of Brahman: in a likeness (*mūrta*) and imageless (*amūrta*). Now the That which is in a likeness is contingent (*asatya*): the That which is imageless, essential (*satya*) Brahman, Light.[91] That Light is the Supernal-Sun.

He verily became with OṀ as Self. He assumed a Trinity (*tredhā*): for the OṀ has three factors, and it is by these that " the whole world is woven, warp and woof, on Him." As it has been said, " Beholding that the Supernal-Sun is OṀ, unify therewith thyself."

And as it has been said, again: " Now, verily, the Chant (*udgītha*) is the Rune (*praṇava*), and the Rune is the Chant; that is indeed the Supernal-Sun, he is the Chant, he OṀ. Thus it says: " The Chant is the Rune, the Inductor (*praṇetra*), image-bearing-light (*bhā-rūpa*), sleepless, unaging, undying, of three feet, three syllables, and again as fivefold known, hid (*nihita*) in the cavern (*guhā*) *of the heart*." For thus it has been said: "The threefold Brahman has his root above; his branches are space, air, fire, water, earth and the other elements.[92] This is called the Single Fig-tree (*eka aśvattha*); and therein inheres the Fiery-Energy (*tejas*) that is the Supernal Sun, and it is likewise of the OṀ. Therefore one should ever laud Him with OṀ, who is the One Enlightener (*eka sambodhayitṛ*).

For it is said, "This Imperishable-Word is as it were profitable, this Imperishable-Word is transcendent; he who knoweth this, whatsoever he desires is his."[92a]

Seventh Prapāṭhaka, 11

This, verily, is the intrinsic-form (*svarūpa*) of the firmament (*nabha*) in the vacance of the inner man (*antarbhūtasya khe*): that is the Supreme Fiery-Energy (*tejas*), determined (*abhihita*) as the Trinity (*tridhā*) of Fire, Supernal-Sun, and Spirit. The intrinsic-aspect of space (*nabha = ākāśa*) in the vacance of the inner man—(*antarbhūtasya khe*) is indeed the Imperishable-Word, OṀ.

And by that Imperishable-Word[92a], the Fiery-Energy sprouts forth (*udbudhyati*), springs-up (*udayati*) and suspires (*ucchvasati*, also "blossoms"): that is verily an everlasting (*ajasram*) basis (*ālamba*) for the vision of Brahman (*brahmadhīya-*). In the spiration (*samīraṇe*) it has its place (*sthāna*) in the dark-heat (*uṣṇa*) that emanates (*prakṣepa*) Light (*prakāśa*), proceeding-upward (*utkramya*) as in the way of smoke when-the-wind-blows (*samīraṇe*), as a branching-forth (*praśākhaya*) in space (*nabha*) the firmament, stem following on stem . . . all-pervading as contemplative vision. . . .[92b]

SIXTH PRAPĀṬHAKA, 35

He who is yonder, yonder Person in the Supernal-Sun—I my-Self am He.

III

THREE VEDIC HYMNS

The Vedas, as we possess them, embody a tradition of immemorial antiquity, already locally developed in characteristic idioms, but by no means original or exclusive to themselves: Veda antedates the Vedas. However, it is not so much intended here to stress this argument, as to point out that there is little or nothing in the metaphysics of the Upaniṣads that necessarily implies a "progress" with respect to the older Vedic books. The "three Vedas" are primarily concerned with "Works" (*karma, yajña*) and with "Genesis" (*bhāva-vṛtta, Bṛhad Devatā*, II, 120[93]; perhaps also *jāta vidyā, Ṛg Veda*, X, 71, 11, and *Nirukta*, I, 8): exegetical matter, such as appears abundantly in the Atharva Veda, Brāhmaṇas, Upaniṣads, and *nirukta* generally, is included amongst the Vedic liturgies only as it were by accident and incidentally. That the language of the Upaniṣads is less archaic than that of the three Vedas proves only a late publication of the traditional exegesis, but in no way proves, nor even suggests to those who recognize the consistency of one tradition in the Vedas and Upaniṣads, that the essential doctrines of the latter had not "always" been taught to those possessed of the necessary qualifications.[94] This would fully accord with the traditional interpretation of "Upaniṣad" as "secret doctrine" or "mystery," *rahasya*, without contradicting the traditional connotation "doctrine with respect to Brahman." In any case, the history of tradition, and the history of literature, are two different things; and that is especially true in India, where even at the present day it is felt that none but a living teacher can communicate ultimate truth.

Furthermore, that is an erroneous view which describes the "beginnings" of Indian "philosophy" as a process of "syncretic" thought, as a "tendency to see that all the angels are really One." On the contrary, Vedic "mythology" as we possess it represents an already "late" and sophisticated stage in the history of symbolism, an employment of increasingly diverse similitudes and images, and of new-found essential names and epithets, accompanied by a tendency towards a conception of these names as those of independent powers, so that a superficial aspect of polytheism is brought about, of the same sort as that which can be recognized in Christianity when it is said with respect to the Trinity, "We do not say *the only God*, for deity is common to several," St. Thomas, *Sum. Th.*, I, Q. 31, A. 2[95]. These elaborations may be regarded from some points of view as a progress in theological science, but from that point of view which takes into consideration that "the angels have fewer ideas and use less means than men," and holds that in a single seeing and in one idea "He" beholds himself and all things simultaneously, and accordingly that with the knowledge of That One "this entire universe becomes known," *Muṇḍaka Up.*, I, 1, 3, rather as a decline. In reality, the notion of a progress or decline is out of place, an absolute progress or decline being no more conceivable in metaphysics than in art: the thing known can only be in the knower according to the mode of the knower,[96] and that is why under changed conditions alternative-formulations (*paryāya*) necessarily present themselves; each of these, in so far as it is "correct," and not in the measure of its complexity or simplicity, expressing one and the same truth. All that concerns the historian of style, rather than the expositor of the meaning of meanings, *paramārtha*: it is precisely with respect to that ultimate significance that *ya evaṁ vidvān* might have been said at any time, and not for the first time when the Upaniṣads were finally " published." A single illustration of this may be cited in the equivalence of Varuṇa, Brahmā-Prajāpati, Viśvakarma, and Nārâyaṇa-Viṣṇu, which can be demonstrated easily from many points of view (cf. *Yakṣas*, II, p. 36). That the Vedic *kavi*[97] was in fact *vidvān* is shown by such well-known assertions as that " The priests speak in divers ways of that which is but one: they call it Agni, Yama, Mātariśvan . . ." *Ṛg Veda*, I, 164, 46; " Priests and singers make manifold the (Sun-) bird that is unique," *ibid.*, X, 114, 5; or when Aditi or Prajāpati are identified with all that is, *ibid.*, I, 89, 10, and X, 121. The ideas and often the actual locutions of the Upaniṣads are to be found in the Vedas, e.g., VI, 16, 35, *yastā vijānat*, equivalent to *ya evam vidvān*; and even more striking, V, 46, 1, *na asyāh vaśmi vimucaṁ na āvṛttaṁ punaḥ, vidvān pathaḥ puraḥ' etā ṛju neśati*, " I covet neither deliverance nor a coming back again, may He that is waywise be my guide and lead me straight," where *punar āvṛttam* can hardly be otherwise understood than in the " later " literature.

A translation of the famous *bhāva vṛtta*, or " Creation hymn," *Ṛg Veda*, X, 129, now follows:

Ṛg Veda, X, 129

" Non-existence (*asat*) then was not, nor Existence (*sat*); neither Firmament (*rajas*), nor Empyrean (*vyoman*) there beyond:

What covered o'er all (*âvarīvar*) and where, or what was *any* resting-place (*śarman*)? What were the Waters (*ambhaḥ*)? Fathomless abyss (*gahanaṁ gaṁbhīram*). 1.

Then was neither death (*mṛtyu*) nor life (*amṛta* nor any fetch (*praketa*) of night or day:

That One breathed (*ānīt*) breathless (*avāta*) by intrinsic-power (*svadhā*), none other was, nor aught there-beyond. 2.

In the beginning (*agre*), Dark-Inert (*tamas*) was hid (*gūḷha*) by Dark-Inert (*tamas*). This all was fluid (*salila*), indeterminate (*apraketa*) :

Void (*tucchi*), by void (*ābhu*) was overlaid (*apihita*) : That One was born (*ajāyat*) by the all-might (*mahi*) of intension (*tapas*). 3.

In the beginning, Will (*kāma*) arose (*samavartat*) therein, the primal seed (*retas*) of Intellect (*manas*), that was the first :

Searching the heart (*hṛd*) throughly by thought (*manīṣā*) wise-singers (*kavayaḥ*) found there the kin (*bandhu*) of Existence (*sat*) in the Non-existent (*asat*). 4.

What trace was stretched across below, and what above ?

Seed (*retas*) was, Allmight (*mahimānaḥ*) was ; Intrinsic-power (*svadhā*) *below*, Purpose (*prayati*) above. 5.

Who knows it aright ? who can here set it forth ? Whence was it born (*ājātā*), whence poured forth (*visṛṭiḥ*)

These Angels (*devāḥ*) are from its pouring-forth (*visarjana*), whence then it came-to-be (*ābabhūva*), who knows ?

Whence outpoured (*visṛṣṭiḥ*) this came to be (*ābabhūva*), or whether one appointed (*dadhe*) it or not,

He who is Over-Eye (*adhyakṣa*) thereof in uttermost Empyrean (*vyoman*), he knows indeed, or knoweth not. 7.

That is what is called a "late" hymn: from our present point of view it suffices that it antedates the earliest Upaniṣads by some centuries. A likeness to Upaniṣadic texts generally, and to our *Bṛhadāraṇyaka Up.*, I, 2, 1, and *Maitri Up.*, V, 2, in particular will be noticed at a glance. This similarity is partly one of verbal identity (*agre, sat, asat, tamas, salila, tapas, kāma, retas, manas, hṛd, tad-eka, ānīt* = *prâṇiti, vāta* = *vāyu, avāta* = *nirvāta, visṛṣṭi, visarjana, etc.*), partly of verbal sense (*ambhaḥ, salila* = *āpah, tapasaḥ-mahi* = *tejas, svadhā* = *māyā, śakti, svabhāva*),[98] and partly of total statement. *Bandhu* (= *sajāta*) "kin" as of blood relationship, is an exceedingly well-found expression for the "opposite relation" of Existence to the Non-existent, God to Godhead, Essence to Nature[99]; as also in *Bṛhadāraṇyaka Up.*, I, 1, 2. As for *rajas*, granted that no more is here directly implied than "firmament" or "space," and that the Sāṁkhya as a formulated system is of later publication,[100] it still remains significant that in our hymn (not to speak of other Vedic sources) we have a trinity of terms (*tamas, rajas*, and *tapasaḥ-mahi* = *tejas* = *sattva*)[101] employed in their correct factorial (*gauṇa*) senses to denote the principles of passivity, movement, and essentiality, "later" represented by the three *guṇas* more explicitly, and by the corresponding Trinity of Viṣṇu, Brahmā, and Śiva. By the "primal seed of Intellect," I understand rather "intellectual virility," "creative intellect," than the *source* of Intellect: cf. *Ṛg Veda* X, 71, 2, *Bṛhadāraṇyaka Up.*, I, 5, 7, and similar passages, where Intellect (*manas*) is the fecundating power that begets upon Utterance or Wisdom (*vāc*). *Amṛta*, in the second stanza, is not "immortality," but simply life, continued existence, as in *Ṛg Veda*, VII, 57, 6, and equivalent to *dīrghamāyuḥ* in X, 85, 19; the sense is "neither birth nor death as yet were."

That "He breathes without air" (*avāta*, cf. later *nirvāṇa*, "despiration") is a profound and significant expression, implying all the correlative of motion without local movement, and the like, which may be properly enunciated of the First Principle, "for (only) where there is a duality, as it were" (*Bṛhadāraṇyaka Up.*, IV, 5, 15) could it be otherwise. The thought is taken up and further developed in several passages of the Upaniṣads, particularly the *Bṛhadāraṇyaka Up.*, as quoted above, p. 46, *Kena Up.*, I, 8, "Know that as Brahman which breathes (*prâṇiti*) without breath (*na . . . prâṇena*) yet by whom breath (*prâṇa*) is breathed (*praṇīyate*)", *Muṇḍaka Up.*, II, 1, 2, and 3, where That from which Intellect (*manas*) and Spiritus (*prâṇa*) are born (*jāyate*) is Itself imageless (*amūrtta*), un-intelligent (*amanassa*), de-spirited (*aprâṇa*), and *Taittirīya Up.*, II, 7, where That without which none might breathe (*prânyāt*) is Self-less (*anātmya*), indiscriminate (*anirukta*), placeless (*anilayana*).

"By intrinsic power" (*svadhā*): cf. *Ṛg Veda*, IV, 13, 5, "by what intrinsic-power (*svadhā*) does he move?" and the answer in I, 144, 2, "When he (as Fire) dwelt diffused in the womb of the Waters (*apāmupasthe*), thence got he (*adhayat*) the intrinsic powers (*svadhāh*) whereby he proceeds (*īyate*)": the Waters, *nirguṇa*-Brahman, unconscious Godhead, being as explained above, the source of all omnipotence (*mahimānaḥ*) and facility (*kauśalya*). Essence being impotent (*stari*) apart from nature; nature being power (*śakti*) and magic (*māyā*), means whereby anything is done.[102] Cf. *Bhagavad Gītā*, IV, 6, "I am born by my own power," where *ātma-māyayā* is clearly the same as *sva-dhayā*, cf. *māyayā* in *Ṛg Veda*, IX, 73, 5 and 9.

"That One" is clearly here not an existence, for

as we have seen, his mode is modeless, in that he breathes without breath: a similar conception is met with in *Ṛg Veda*, I, 164, 4, where That "which supports Him who is by way of being the first born embodiment," *prathamaṁ jāya-mānam-asthanvantam* . . . *vibharti*, is itself "bodiless," or more literally, "boneless," *anasthā*, that is to say, "structureless." 'That" is not yet "Selfed" (*ātmanvī*)—"before creatures were, God was not God, albeit he was Godhead," Eckhart, I, 410. *Tamas* (as in *Maitri Up.*, V. 2), *apraketa salila, gahanaṁ gambhīra*, etc., are all terms naturally designating the undifferentiated, unintelligible Godhead, "which is as though it were not," Eckhart, I, 381: *asat*, non-existent, *gūḷha*, hidden, there where "darkness reigns in the unknown known unity," Eckhart, I, 368, Cf. p. 6 and Note 21.

"What covered o'er?" That is, what and where was the world? *āvarīvar* being from *varī*, intensive reduplicated form of *vṛ*, "to cover," "veil." The world is thought of as veiling the ultimate reality, cf. *Ṛg Veda*, V, 19, 1, "state after state is generated, veil (*vavri*) from veil appears," hence also the prayer, *Maitri Up.*, VI, 35, with respect to the Sun, "That face do thou unveil (*apāvṛṇu*)" or "That door do thou open."

Our hymn is by no means necessarily an expression of scepticism: it is rather wonder than a wondering that is suggested. "Who knows" is no more "sceptical" than Kabīr's *tāsukā soi santa jānai*, "who are the Comprehensors thereof?" or Blake's "Did he who made the lamb make thee?" "He knows or knows not," if understood to mean "he knows *and* knows not" would be sound theology. In the last stanza, alternative theories of "emanation" and of "creation by design" are propounded.[103] In any case, the very form of the various statements and questions proves that sound ontological speculation was by no means a new thing, for it is inconceivable that such questions had been correctly formulated just a week or year before this particular hymn was published.

Not only are the terms and implications of our hymn all formally correct (*pramiti*), they tally also in form and content with those of the Upaniṣads. Yet we are asked to believe that Vedic thought was "primitive"[104]—that the wise-singers of the Vedic hymns were able to express themselves in terms that have been universally employed elsewhere and otherwhen with a deep and known significance, and all without knowing what it was they said. It is as though it were argued that the law of gravity had been hit upon by lucky chance, long before anyone had consciously observed that heavy objects have a tendency to fall. Surely our faith in uniformity forbids us to imagine, what is outside the range of our experience, viz., that any sound formula, any clear statement of principles, could have been propounded by anyone who did not understand his own words.[105] It would be far easier to suppose that such a statement had been propounded in the past by those who knew what they were saying, and that it had since come to be repeated mechanically without understanding: but on the one hand, that would be to push the beginnings of wisdom too far back for the comfort of those who fondly believe that wisdom came into the world only in their own day, and on the other would need proof by some internal evidence of the presumed misunderstanding. I prefer to believe that wherever and whenever a proposition has been correctly and intelligibly stated (and that covers both verbal and visual symbolisms, both "scripture" and "art") the proposition was also understood. Problems of ontology are not so simple that they can be solved by "luck" or "inspiration": on the contrary there is no sort of work more arduous than "audition," and here a man has need of all the power of the pure intellect.

A version now follows of another hymn of creation, *Ṛg Veda*, X, 72:

Ṛg Veda, X, 72

"Now shall we tell clearly of the kindred (*jānā*) of the Angels (*deva*),
As it may be seen in the chanted songs, and of a transcendental aeon (*uttare yuge*). 1.
The Lord-of-Increase (Brahmaṇaspati) like a smith with-his-bellows-smithied (*adhamat*) it;
In the primordial aeon (*pūrvye yuge*) of the Angels was Existence (*sat*) from the Non-existent (*asat*) born (*ajāyat*). 2.
In the primordial aeon (*prathame yuge*) of the Angels, the Existent was from the Non-existent born,
And therewith the Airts (*āśāḥ*), that was from the Recumbent (*uttānapad*). 3.
From the Recumbent was born the Earth (*bhūr*), from Earth the Airts born:
Dakṣa (Pure-Act) from Aditi (the In-finite) born, and Aditi from Dakṣa. 4.
Aditi, verily, was born, She is thy daughter, Dakṣa!
From thee again were born the Angels, the Blest, the King of Immortality. 5.
As ye Angels stood-firm (*atiṣṭha*) there in the Flood (*salila*), each-enlinked-with-other (*su-saṁrabdha*).
There as it were *from the feet* of dancers (*nṛtyatām*) rose the pungent (*tīvra*) dust (*reṇu*). 6.
When ye, O Angels, together with the Disponents (*yatayaḥ*), expanded (*apinvata*) the *Three* Worlds (*bhuvanāni*)

Then brought-ye-to-birth in the Sea (*samudra*) the hidden (*gūḷha*) Sun (*sūrya*). 7.
Eight are the sons of the In-finite (Aditi) of embodied birth (*jātaḥ tanvaḥ*) :
With seven She went upward to the Angels, the Sun-bird (Mārtāṇḍa) She left here. 8.
With seven Sons the In-finite (Aditi) fared upward to the primordial aeon (*pūrvyaṁ yugam*),
The Sun-bird She bore-hither (*ābharat*) unto repeated birth and death (*prajāyai mṛtyave*). 9.

As pointed out by Charpentier, from whose version (*Suparṇasage*, pp. 386-388) the foregoing differs only in minor details, this hymn describes creation as primarily from the " Recumbent," and secondarily the terms of the stirring of the Waters by the feet of angelic dancers in a ring. That is a figure closely related to, though not identical with that of the Churning of the Ocean, the Epic *samudra manthana*. And as in some other accounts of the beginning, the dust or spray arising from the troubled Waters becomes the Earth, the support of living beings amidst the possibilities of existence.

The " Recumbent "[106] is originally Varuṇa, " great Yakṣa supported on the back of the Waters," *Atharva Veda*, X, 7, 38, from whose navel rises the Tree of Life, and therein are the Angelic Host (*viśve devāḥ*) ; later, Brahma, finally Nārâyaṇa-Viṣṇu. That he reclines supported in the Waters corresponds to the reflection of his image in the Waters, as described in *Pañcaviṁśa Brāhmaṇa*, VII, 8, 1, cited above, p. 8. In that reciprocal sense, he as Dakṣa is " born " of Aditi, that is as a reflected image, and Aditi of Dakṣa inasmuch as the Waters antecedent to his shining, his knowledge, are but an unrevealed possibility. Dakṣa, " Operation," " Skill," the

" right hand " of God, Dante's *puro atto*, being an essential name, like Viśvakarma and Prajāpati, is rightly identified with Prajāpati, *Śatapatha Brāhmaṇa*, II, 4, 4, 2.[107]

To render rightly the familiar words *sat* and *asat* is far more difficult than might appear at first sight. In certain passages, *Bṛhadāraṇyaka Up.*, I, 4, 1, and *Chāndogya Up.*, VI, 2, 2, the relativity of Existence to a permissive cause (Non-existence) is ignored or rejected, Self (*ātman*), Person (*puruṣa*), Existence (*sat*) being taken for granted as first cause. In our text and many others, e.g., *Ṛg Veda*, X, 129, 1, *Bṛhadāraṇyaka Up.*, V, 2, 1, *Chāndogya Up.*, II, 2, 1, *Taittirīya Up.*, what is meant by the birth of *sat* from *asat* may be the birth of Intellect, Self, Person, Consciousness, from Death, Privation, Dark-Inert, Unconsciousness ; of God from Godhead, essence from nature, [108] cf. Dakṣa from Aditi. In general, however, *sat* has the more restricted sense " that which exists " or " is actual," so, for example, Sāyaṇa on *Ṛg Veda*, VII, 87, 6, equates *sat* with *jagat*, the " world," literally " that which moves " (of course, with reference to local movement). A very clear distinction of *sat* from *asat* occurs in *Atharva Veda*, X, 7, 21, " The kindreds (sc. of the Angels) understand (*viduḥ*) the branch (*śakham*, i.e., the Tree of Life, *praśākhaya* of Maitri Up., VII, 11) established (*pratiṣṭhantīm*, i.e., in the Waters as the manifest existence of all things) by-way-of (*iva*) Non-Existence (*asat*) ; those-here-below (*avare*) who revere (*upâsate*) the Branch reckon-it (*manyante*) as Actuality (*sat*)." Here, as so often happens, the inverse points of view, angelic and human, metaphysical-intellectual (*parokṣa*) and empirical-sensational (*pratyakṣa*) are expressly contrasted ; the distinction of the verbal roots *vid* and *man*, implying respectively " knowledge " and " opinion," should be noted, and it is hard to see why Whitney should have found the stanza " highly obscure." Corresponding to these uses of *sat* as " real " or " actual " or " actual " (as realia are "real"), or "actually existing," is that of *sattva* as tension in relation to *tamas* as relaxation, and also that of *sattva* as equivalent to *bhūta*, "living being," "mortal" (whose existence depends on the maintenance of a tension). *Yat prameyam tat sat*.

In the *Ṛg Veda* generally, *satya* = *ṛta*, the Law or Way of Heaven, and hence also "Truth." In the same way in *Taittirīya Up.*, II, 6, *satya* is contrasted with *anṛta*, and quite consistently, in *Maitri Up.*, VI, 3, *asatya* corresponds to *sat* in *Bṛhadāraṇyaka Up.*, II, 3. In the Upaniṣads *passim*, *satya* is equated with Brahman, Prathama Yakṣa, Ātman. Puruṣa, Prajāpati, Prâṇa, Āditya, Arka, etc., that is to say with God as he is in himself and as he manifests: e.g., *Maitri Up.*, VI, 6, where Prajāpati as *satya* thence proceeds to utterance of the grosser world-forms. The symbol *satya* has thus a reference quite distinct from that of *sat*; but it will be found that its reference includes and further illuminates that of *sat* [109]. That is evident from *Bṛhadāraṇyaka Up.*, V, 5, 1, "The Waters (*āpaḥ*) poured forth (*asṛjata*) Essence (*satya*); Essence, Brahman; Brahman, Prajāpati; Prajāpati; Prajāpati, the (Several) Angels"; and is developed even more clearly when the reference is analysed, as in *ibid.* II, 3, where *-tya* corresponds to the notion of *asat*: here the Brahman in a likeness (*mūrta*),[110] mortal (*martya*), existent (*sthita*)[111] is *sat*, "actual," while the imageless (*amūrta*) Brahman, not-mortal (*amṛta*), immanent-and-universal (*yat*), is "yonder" or "infinite (*-tya*), cf. Rāmānuja's glosses *yadvyāpakam* and *tyattaditaradityarthaḥ*. In some cases the meaning is emphasized by the use of the expression *satyasya satyam*, e.g., *ibid.*, II, 3, 6, and *Aitareya Āraṇyaka*, II, 1, 5, and II, 3, 8, where That (Brahman) "in which is yoked the ultimate reality, there it is that all the Angels become One." It would appear then that *sat* must be distinguished from *asat* not as "Being" from "Non-being," but rather as "Existence" from "Non-existence";

i.e., from Being *and* Non-being, which are not existent but are the possibilities of Existence.

The Vedic doctrine of Angels has never been seriously studied.[112] "Because of His great-Plenitude-and-Majesty (*mahā-bhāgya*) they apply many names to him who is single (*ekaika*)," *Nirukta*, VII, 4. "Because of their Great-Self-hood (*mahâtmya*) a diversity of names is given to the three angels, Agni, Indra-and-Vāyu, Sūrya, here, betwixt, and in the Empyrean, apparent in this or that (world), according to the ordering-of-their-stations (*sthāna-vibhāga*). To wit that they are powers (*vibhūti*) their names are different. The wise-singers in their formulæ, however, say that they have a mutual origin (*anyonyayonitā*, cf. *itaretarajanmāna* in *Nirukta*, VII, 4).[113] These angels are called by different names according to their spheres. Some say that they belong (*bhakta*) thereto and are mainly concerned therewith: but Self (*ātman*, i.e., Person) is rightly-predicated as the whole (i.e., only) distributive-assumption (*bhakta*) on the part of those three foremost Lords of the World who have been separately mentioned above. They say that the weapon (*ayudha*) or vehicle (*vāhana*) of any (angel) are his fiery-energy (*tejas*).[114] Likewise Wisdom (*vāc*) is separately lauded as of this (sphere), as of Indra's (midmost), and as heavenly.[115] In all those lauds which are addressed to many angels (*bahudevatā*), and in those joint lauds which are in the dual, the (three aforesaid) Lords are predominant," *Bṛhad Devatā*, I, 69-75, of *Nirukta*, VII, 4 and 5, where the Angels are also "members" (*aṅga*) of the Self, and *Ṛg Veda*, V, 3, 1, where the Several Angels are "in Him" who is variously designated as Agni, Varuṇa, Mitra, and Indra.

So far, then, it is clear that the Angels spoken of are the Selves or Persons of the Trinity (*tridhā*, see above, p. 13f.): either designated as already mentioned, or by whatever alternative essential or personal names may be employed, as Āditya, Prâṇa, Prajāpati, Dakṣa, Mitra-Varunna, Agni,

Brahmā, Viṣṇu, Śiva, etc. To these will correspond, of course, alternative essential or personal names of Wisdom (*vāc*), such as Prakṛti, Māyā, Urvaśī, Sarasvatī, Śrī-Lakṣmī, Durgā, etc. It is just these *bahudevatā*, the *daivasya dhāman* = *devāḥ* of *Ṛg Veda*, VII, 58, 1, *viśve yajatrāḥ* of *Ṛg Veda*, I, 65, the "birds-of-a-feather" or "fellow-nestlings" (*nīḷayaḥ*) of *Ṛg Veda*, X, 92, 6, the *sarva daivatya* of *Bṛhadāraṇyaka Up.*, I, 2, 7, who are the Viśve Devāh, "Several Angels," or "Angelic Host" in a special sense, who are so constantly lauded in the Vedas, e.g., *Ṛg Veda*, X, 82, 5, and *Atharva Veda*, X, 7, 38: also the same as the unspecified "Angels" when these are mentioned as already present "in the beginning," or as co-operating in the "first sacrifice," as in *Ṛg Veda*, X, 90 and 129, as well as X, 72, where "born" (*anvajāyanta*) must be taken in connection with *susaṁrabdha*, and with respect to such terms as *ekajātatva* and *itaretarajanmāna* cited above, to mean "connascent" rather than eventfully born. So far as our text is concerned then, the Angels mentioned are to be regarded as those of one, viz., the premier or super-celestial order, that of the Āditya-maṇḍala: an order everlasting with respect to time, as recognized in the *Pañcaviṁśa Brāhmaṇa*, VI, 9, 15 f., where the Angels are spoken of as a "first emanation" (*prathamam asṛgram*) and "enduring utterance" (*sthita vyāhṛtiḥ*) and contrasted in this respect with the coming into existence of rational beings (*mānuṣyaḥ*, "men," "mortals") whose utterance is "from day to day." We say "order" rather than hierarchy advisedly, because the arrangement (*dhā*, *saṁhitā*) of the Persons represents a natural or logical, not a hierarchical order; there is no precedence here.[116]

The mention of Yatis, here rendered "Disponents" according to the root meaning, is of special interest: their co-presence with the Several Angels antecedent to local motion is implied. These "ascetics" are evidently the same as the "Prophets" (*ṛṣayaḥ*) of other texts, who together with the Patriarchs (*pitaraḥ*) are desirous of progeny (*prajākāmya*, *Praśna Up.*, I, 9). The return (*punar āvṛtti*) of Prophets and Patriarchs alike from the *pitṛyāna*[117] course to corporeal (*śarīraka*) existence in a future aeon (*yuga*, *kalpa*) is determined by the unexpended force of former works, in other words the Prophets and Patriarchs are the bearers of heredity. The One Angel or Several Angels are the givers of Life: but it is Man, "Adam," "Āyu," who bestows upon every existence its specific character. Brahmā-Prajāpati in relation to the world is himself a Patriarch in this sense, his "Works" (*karma*) or "Sacrifice" (*yajña*)[118] in any aeon determining his re-embodiment at the dawn of a succeeding cycle.

In the Epic account of the Churning of the Ocean, we find instead of the Yatis, Angels and Asuras pulling in opposite directions. That by no means implies an equation of Yatis with Asuras, but rather a different imagery, in which the Yatis as bearers of heredity are replaced by Angels *and* Demons: the latter collectively representing the good and evil factors (*dharmâdharmau*) and all other pairs of opposites (*dvandvau*)[119] which are essential to the existence of a perceptible universe, though they have no place, as such, in the "invisible." As we have seen above, the Lord of Life (*īśānaḥ amṛtasya*, *Ṛg Veda*, X, 90, 2), who bids us but be, acts as permissive, not as immediate cause of the operation of the conflicting principles[120]: these contending glories, the children and disciples of Prajāpati (*Bṛhadāraṇyaka Up.*, V, 2), are the immediate cause of idiosyncrasy in living beings. All that corresponds to what is called in Christianity "original sin," Bōhme's "turba": for it should not be overlooked that the consequence of "original sin," viz., the loss of innocence, is not especially the knowledge of evil, but precisely the "knowledge of good *and* evil."

"Then brought ye to birth in the Sea the hidden Sun": that would be the same as Agni's often mentioned birth in the Waters, where he lies hidden (i.e., not yet reflected in a counter-shining) until sought for and discovered by the Several Angels. The innumerable Vedic allusions to the finding of the Sun or Fire, lost in the Waters, in the Depths (*guhā*), or in the Darkness (*tamas*)—e.g., *Ṛg Veda*, V, 40, 6, *gūḷhaṁ sūryaṁ tamasâpavratena*—have primary reference to the obscuration of Light antecedent to the Dawn of a World-cycle, and to the finding of this Light by means of hymns or rites chanted or undertaken by Angels or men. Naturally enough the analogous rites are performed, and the same hymns are chanted at the dawn of every day, or during an eclipse, to effect the return of the hidden Light. But it must not be overlooked that the Waters, the Depths, and the Darkness, are also the Depths of the Heart, and that for him who understands, the same hymns and rites are means to the inward vision of that Supernal Sun of which the shining and the darkness are without succession, nor subject to any accident of time.

Of the begotten of Aditi, "Children of the Liberty," viz., the well-known group of the Eight Ādityas, it is said that seven return upwards, that would be by the *devayāna* to the source of their being: while one remains in the world, the manifested Sun in each of the Three Worlds, subject to mortality.[121] Here then it is said that one-eighth of deity taking on mortality, remains incarnate in the universe: elsewhere we find a statement that only one-quarter of him is present here. Such expressions must not be understood to imply a partibility of *being*, but only the incommensurability of the incalculable totality of existences in time with the infinite unity of being in eternity.

We have rendered *yuga* as "aeon" with intentional regard to the dual meaning of this word as (1) a great period of time, and (2) a power existing from eternity, in and of the Pleroma.[122] But in our three hymns, *pūrvya yuga*, *uttara yuga*, etc., denote as much a place beyond place, Eternity quâ place, as an ancient lineage (Charpentier's *alt Geschlecht*), or a time beyond time: *pūrvya yuga* is really *vyoman*, "the motionless heaven, this firmament is the abode of the blest", Eckhart, I, 170, and that "beyond" is in the lotus of the heart, the locus of space-in-itself (*ākāśa*, *Maitri Up.*, VI, 2), "all is contained therein," *Chāndogya Up.*, VIII, 3, "he who knows Brahman hid (*nihitam*) in the cavern-of-the-heart (*guhāyam*), in the uttermost Empyrean (*parame vyoman*), he wins all desires and therewith also Brahman," *Taittirīya Up.*, II, 1, cf. *brahmaṁ pūrvyam*, *Śvetâśvatara Up.*, II, 5 and 7. Other terms having a reference similar to that of "Pleroma" include *purīṣa* and *purīṣin* in *Ṛg Veda*, I, 163, 1, and I, 164, 12; *bhūmān* in *Chāndogya Up.*, VII, 23 and 24; and *pūrṇa apravartin* in *Kauṣītaki Up.*, IV, 8.

That ancient supercelestial place, kindred, and time are contrasted with the realms of birth and death, the Three Worlds, as enduring not merely for a time, but until the end of time; there are the Persons, the Angels, and the Saints, an immortal kin, *amṛta-bandhavaḥ*, thence there is no return (*punar āvṛtti*), no gliding down (*avaprabhraṁśaṇa, avasarpaṇa*); though this is not the Unity of the Persons, not an absolute immortality but rather a *sthayitā* of incalculable duration, not out of, but throughout, time. This is in fact Paradise, the Paradise beyond the Sun, accessible to the Comprehensors only: originally Varuṇa's (*Jaiminīya Brāhmaṇa*, I, 42-44), later Brahmā's (*Kauṣītaki Up.*, I, 2-7), still later also Amitâbha's (*Sukhāvatī Sūtra*).

Accordingly, at least in passages where this primordial angelic sphere is clearly implied by the context, we ought to render terms such as *vyoman*, *dyauḥ*, *divi*, *nāka*, and even *yuga*[128] by "Empyrean," "Paradise" or "Pleroma," rather than as "heaven." For whereas Brahmā's Paradise lies beyond the Sun, beyond the gateway of the worlds (*loka-dvāra*, *Chāndogya*, VIII, 6, 5) whereby there is forwarding only for the Comprehensor (*vidu*), *ibid.*, Indra's heaven is but the uppermost of the Three Worlds, a heaven accessible to all who have done good works, irrespective of understanding, and whence there is for them a constant coming back to terrestrial conditions.

Ṛg Veda, X, 90

The Person (Puruṣa) has a thousand eyes, a thousand heads, a thousand feet :
Encompassing (*vṛtvā*) Earth (*bhūmim*) on every side, he rules (*vṛtvā*) firmly-established (*atyatiṣṭhat*) in the heart (*daśaṅgulam*). 1.
The Person, too, is all This, both what has been (*bhūtam*) and what is to come (*bhavyam*),
Even the Lord (*īśānaḥ*) of Life (*amṛtasya*) when he rises-up (*atirohati*) by food (*annena*). 2.
Great as the Omnipotence (*mahimā*) thereof may be, greater yet than that is the Person :
One fourth of him is all-existences (*viśva-bhūtāni*), three-fourths in the Empyrean (*divi*) undying (*amṛtam*). 3.
With three parts the Person is above (*ūrdhvaḥ*), but one part came-into-existence (*abhavat*) here :
Thence he proceeded (*vyakrāmat*) everywhere, regarding Earth and Heaven (*sāśanānaśane*). 4.
Of him was Nature (*Virāj*) born (*ajāyat*), from Nature Person born :
When born, he ranges (*atyaricyat*) Earth (*bhūmi*) from East (*paścād*) to West (*puraḥ*). 5.
Whenas the Angels laid-out the sacrifice (*yajñam-atanvat*) with the Person for their offering (*havi*),

Spring was the oil, Summer the fuel, Autumn the offering. 6.

Him, erst-born Person, they besprinkled on the strew (*barhiṣi*) :

The Angels, the Saints (*sādhyāḥ*) and the Prophets (*ṛṣayaḥ*) by him made sacrifice. 7.

From that sacrifice, when the offering was all accomplished, the speckled oil was gathered up :

That made the birds and beasts of field and forest. 8.

From that sacrifice, when the offering was all accomplished, the Verses (*Ṛg*) and Liturgies (*Sāma*) were born (*jajñire*),

The Metres, and the Formulary (*Yajur*) born (*ajāyat*) of it. 9.

Therefrom were born horses, and whatso *beasts* have *cutting* teeth in both jaws.

Therefrom were born cows, and therefrom goats and sheep. 10.

When they divided (*vyadadhuḥ*) the Person, how-many-fold (*katidhā*) did they arrange (*vyakalpayan*) him ?[124]

What was his mouth ? what were his arms ? how were his thighs and feet named (*ucyate*) ? 11.

The Priest (*Brāhmaṇa*) was his mouth ; of his arms was made (*kṛtaḥ*) the Ruler (Rājanya) ;

His thighs were the Merchant-folk (Vaiśya) ; from his feet was born the Servant (Śudra). 12.

The Moon (Candramā) was born from his Intellect (*manas*) ; the Sun (Sūrya) from his eye ;

From his mouth the King (Indra) and Fire (Agni) ; from his Breath (*prâṇa*) Wind (*Vāyu*). 13.

From his navel (*nābhyaḥ*) was the Firmament (*antarikṣam*) ; from his head was turned-out (*samavartat*) Heaven (*dhyauḥ*) ;

From his feet the Earth (*bhūmiḥ*) : the Airts (*diśaḥ*) from his ear : so they designed (*akalpayan*) the *Three* Worlds (*lokān*). 14.

With a sacrifice the Angels sacrificed unto the Sacrifice ; there were established the first Laws *prathamāni dharmāṇi*) :

These Almighty-powers (*mahimānaḥ*) abide in (*sacanta*) the Empyrean (*nākam*) from of old (*pūrve*) ; there are the Saints (*sādhyāḥ*), the Angels. 16.

This text, translated nearly in accordance with Professor Brown's admirable version in J.A.O.S., 51, 108-118, requires but little additional comment. " Rises up by food," i.e., " exists," *tiṣthati*. It follows that *amrta* is not here " immortality," but simply " life," as also in X, 90, 2, where " life " and " death " are complementary aspects of mortality : in the same way we have seen that " death " (*mṛtyu*) may be either Death-absolute, the same as Immortality-absolute, or may be " death " as the complement to " life " and " death."

The second half of the first verse clearly enunciates the same thought as that which finds expression in the *Maitri Up.*, VI, 1, that of the exact correspondence of the outer and the inner tracks of the Self ; and this tends to confirm the traditional explanation of *daśaṅgulam* as " heart."[125] With this curious term may be compared various measurements of the Self in the heart, mentioned in the Upaniṣads. For example, the second half of our verse 1 is literally repeated in *Śvetâśvatara Up.*, III, 14, preceded by stanzas in which he, Puruṣa and inner-Self, is said to be *aṅguṣṭha-mātrā*, "of the measure of a thumb," cf. *Kaṭha Up.*, IV, 12, and VI, 17, and *Chāndogya Up.*, V, 18. Again, in the *Śvetâśvatara Up.*, III, 20 and V, 9, we find *anoraṇīyān mahatomahīyāt*, "less than atomic, greater than magnitude," and *vālâgra-śatabhāgasya śatadhā*, combined with *ananta*, that is "a hundredth part of the hundredth part of the point of a hair," and yet "without end." All these fanciful measurements applied to the Self abiding in the heart are tantamount to "undimensioned," and that is what is really meant: "so subtle is the nature of the soul that space might not exist at all for all it troubles her," Eckhart, I, 279.

As to the Perfected, the Saints, *sādhyāḥ*, the *siddhāḥ* of later texts: these are to be understood, as rightly explained by Sāyaṇa,[126] to be those who have long ago by knowledge or devotion passed through the gateway of the Three Worlds to the Empyrean paradise there beyond, whence there is no return[127] and are now abiding there as Angelic Powers: perhaps to be identified with the Yatis of X, 72, 7, and in any case partaking in the work of creation. Just as in Christianity, "men can merit glory in such a degree as to be equal to the angels, in each of the angelic grades; and this implies that men are taken up into the orders of the angels," St. Thomas, *Sum. Th.*, I, Q. 108, A.8: and "the man who is exalted above time into eternity will do with God what he did in the past and also what he does in the next thousand years .... meaning that in eternity, exalted above time, man does one work with God . . . works wrought by thee there are all living," Eckhart, I, 150, 151, "God made the universe and I with him, standing as I did all undefined albeit substantial in the Father," I, 398. In *Ṛg Veda*, I, 164, 50, the Sādhyas are *pūrve devāḥ*, "Angels from aforetime"; and as explained in the Appendix, *sādhya* = *muni*. The Sādhya is thus more than a saint: they are Sādhyas who in a former æon have become the Light of the World, the Pillar of the Universe. The notion corresponds to that of "former Buddhas," or Agni's "elder brothers" in x, 51, 6.

It will be observed that the Brahman here (v. 12) takes precedence of the Kṣatriya. We know that there existed in ancient India a conflict on this point. A very remarkable solution is offered in the *Bṛhadāraṇyaka Up.*, I, 4, 11, where the spirit-power (*brahma*) is said to be the source (*yoni*) of the temporal power, than which there is nothing higher: in other words, the spiritual power is to the temporal power as Being to Existence, as Unconscious (super-conscious) to conscious, the conscious naturally having worldly precedence. Cf. "The lower heart moves like a strong, powerful commander who despises the heavenly ruler because of his weakness, and has seized for himself the leadership of the affairs of state," Lü Tzü in Wilhelm and Jung, *Secret of the Golden Flower*, p. 27. It is precisely from this point of view that the character of Indra can be best explained: the original Indra (an aspect of Agni, *Ṛg Veda*, V, 3, 1, and born of truth, *ibid.*, IV, 19, 2) representing the legitimate Temporal Power (*kṣatra*), in relation to Agni or Vāyu (Prâṇa) as Spiritual Power (*brahma*); the "fallen" Indra ("deluded," *Bṛhad Devatā*, VII, 54) self-infatuated, misconceiving his position, and asserting his independence, as in *Ṛg Veda*, IV, 142 and X, 124.

We have rendered Indra tentatively as "king," assuming that *indra, devānām indra*, was originally, that would be antecedent to the Vedas as we possess them, an essential name[128] of him who is but One, not an independent deity of alien ethnic origin, as has generally been thought.[129] His treatment as a separate and rival deity, often displacing Varuṇa, would thus afford an ancient parallel to such cases as those of Kāmadeva who are properly speaking "powers" of Varuṇa or Brahman, only later or popularly worshipped as independent persons: Śrī-Lakṣmī presenting a similar case on the Mother-side. It is noteworthy that in the *Bṛhad Devatā*, I, 69, and *Nirukta*, VII, 5, where the Trinity consists of Agni, Indra and Vāyu, and Āditya, Indra and Vāyu count as one person[130]: in the *Bṛhadāraṇyaka Up.*, IV, 2, 2, Indra is interpreted as "Kindler" and as correlative to Virāj, "their place of conjunction is the space in the heart," *ibid.*, 3; in *Taittirīya Up.*, I, 6, 1.

Indra is "individuality." The accepted etymology connects *indra* with *ind* "to drop," and *indu* "drop" (especially a drop of *soma*[131]) or mathematical point, cf. *bindu*, *parabindu*, which "point" in *yantra* symbolism[132] represents the I-ness, "I am," *ahaṁkāra*, *abhimānatva*, "egoity" in Deity, and subjectivity generally. Indra, and Indra's rather childish character become indeed most intelligible when he is thus regarded as a personification of the ego-principle, *aham, abhimāna*. That ego-principle in Deity, set up as an independent person, and usurping many of the divine functions, could have developed only as (1) the king of an inferior heaven, or (2) as a demon deliberately laying claim to the supernal throne. The latter development seems to have taken place in Christianity, in the case of Lucifer-Satan, and likewise in the *Avesta*, where Indra and *daeva* are demonic powers[133] (cf. *Bṛhad Devatā*, VII, 54, "having obtained sovereignty amongst the Daityas, puffed up with pride by reason of his titan-magic (*asura-māyā*) he began to harass the Angels"). The former development took place in India, though even here it may be observed that Indra constantly appears in the guise of a Tempter, jealous of his throne, and sending his nymphs to lead astray the saints on earth who might displace him.[134] None but the warlike and arrogant Indra introduces elements of discord: in IV, 30, 3-5, he is represented as fighting against the heavenly powers, and it is only by theft or purchase that he gets possession of the heavenly *soma* which was originally Varuṇa's and guarded by the Gandharva Viśvavāsu or Kṛśānu (IV, 27, 3). In any case, and already in the Ṛg Veda, Indra is wholly an angel of *this* world.[135] In effect, Indra in Brahmanical mythology plays that part which is allotted to Māra (Kāmadeva) in Buddhism.

NOTES

1 " One of our most ancient philosophers who found the truth long, long before God's birth, ere ever there was Christian faith at all as it is now, Eckhart, I, 103. Cf. Note 58.

2 Except where otherwise stated, references to Eckhart are to C. de B. Evans' admirable version in two volumes, London, 1924.

3 On the one hand, the professional scholar, who has direct access to the sources, functions in isolation: on the other, the amateur propagandist of Indian thought disseminates mistaken notions. Between the two, no provision is made for the educated man of good will.

4 Langdon, S., *Tammuz and Ishtar*, Oxford, 1914, p.v.

5 It is not without good reason that Jahāngīr speaks of " the science of the Vedanta which is the science of Sufism," *Tuzuk-i-Jahāngīrī*, translated by Rogers and Beveridge, I, p. 356. Parallels to almost all the ideas discussed below could be adduced from Islamic theology: see especially Nicholson, R.A., *Studies in Islamic mysticism*, 1921, and Macdonald, D.B., *The development of the idea of spirit in Islam*, Acta Orientalia, IX, 1931. It may be noted that the ontology of a non-Christian tradition has been competently discussed by these authors in a way that has never been attempted by any professional European student of the Vedas.

6 A distinction of existence from pure being is easily made: " being " in itself is modeless, " existence " is being in a mode. Essence and nature, *per se*, are evidently non-existent: it need scarcely be added that this " non-existence," viz., the absence of properties, has nothing in common with the non-existence of the absurd or self-contradictory, for example, a square circle; it is not illogical, but alogical, or ineffable, all that can be said of it being purely analogical. Nevertheless, the practical use of the terms Non-being, Being, and Existence, presents real difficulties.

We understand Non-being and Being to be correlative aspects, the inseparable Nature and Essence, of Brahman, the Supreme Identity, not yet existent, antecedent to procession, *solus ante principium*, *apravartin*, *Kauṣītaki Up.*, IV, 8: and understand Existence to include all multiplicity, whether nominal and informal, or real and formal. Non-being is the permissive principle, first cause, of Being: Being the permissive principle, first cause, of Existence. Thus:

Asat	Non-being (*avyakta*)	*anātmya*	*nirguṇa, amūrta, akāla*:	Brahman, *satya*
	Being (*vyakt-āvyakta*)	*param-ātman*		
Sat	Existence (*vyakta*)	*pratyag-ātman* (Visve Devāḥ, *viśvā bhuvanāni*)	*saguṇa, mūrta, kāla, sthita, martya*	

It follows that *asat* can be rendered correctly either as Non-being or as Non-existence: *sat* either as Being or as Existence, as may best suit the context. The problem arises only in connection with "Being": if we render *asat* and *sat* as Non-being and Being, then, *sat* must cover both Being in itself and Being in a mode. The terms are further discussed below, p. 102.

[7] Not that these are commensurable terms: Theistic and Nihilistic points of view are partial, and therefore in apparent opposition, as for example in the case of Śaivism and Buddhism; while Metaphysics, *jñāna-vāda*, underlies, justifies, and embraces all other points of view.

[8] From the Vedic point of view, "angelology" would be more accurate.

[9] On this "kinship" depends the "incestuous" character of so many myths of creation. It should be observed that the term "myth" properly implies the symbolic (verbal, iconographic or dramatic) representation of the operation of power or energy: protons and electrons in this sense are "mythical" beings. A myth, such as the Grail myth, or the Birth of Brahmā, is neither a "fairy tale" nor a "mystery" *in the modern sense* of the words, but simply a presentation. He who regards the myth or icon as a statement of fact, and he who regards it as fantasy, are equally misled: myth is to history as universal to particular, *raison d'être* to *l'être*; icon to species as exemplar to instance. Symbolism and imagery (*pratīka, pratibimba*, etc.), the purest form of art, is the proper language of metaphysics: "the symbol always presupposes that the chosen expression is the best possible description, or formula, of a relatively unknown fact . . . which is none the less known or postulated as existing." (Jung). Traditional symbolism is also more nearly a universal language than any other; the greater part of its idiom is the common property and inheritance of nearly all peoples, and can be traced back at least to the fifth or sixth millennium B.C. (cf. Winckler, *Die babylonische Geisteskultur*, 1907, Jeremias, *Handbuch des altorientalischen geisteskultur*, 1929, and Langdon, *Semitic mythology*, 1931), and to the beginnings of agriculture or there beyond.

[10] Cf. "He hath brought me forth His son in the image of His eternal fatherhood, that I should also be a father and bring forth Him," Eckhart, Claud Field's *Sermons*, p. 26; cf. Jīlī, cited by Nicholson, *Studies* . . . p. 112, "I am the child whose father is his son, and the wine whose vine is its jar. . . . I met the mothers who bore me, and I asked them in marriage, and they let me marry them." "The Snake's Bull-Father—the Bull's Father-snake" is cited by Harrison, *Prolegomena* . . . p. 495, from frg. ap. Clem(ent) of Al(exandria). *Protr.*, I, 2, 12. Or again, of Agni, "being the Son of the Angels, thou hast become their Father," *Ṛg Veda*, I, 69, 1: Agni is the "father of his father," *ibid.*, VI, 16, 35, and "whoever understands this (*yastā vijānat*) is his father's father," i.e., surpasses his father.

[11] Also, of course, in science, "philosophy," psychology, and other "practical" disciplines.

[12] Hence the constant use of essential names common to both, a certain indistinction of Father and Son, the distinction of Person being lost in their unity of Godhead, of the common nature.

[13] Thus, antecedent to procession:

Person (Father)—Spirit (Will)—Nature (Mother)

and posterior to procession:

NOTES

Person (Father)—Nature (Mother)
\Spirit (Son, Life)/

14 See Böhme, *Mysterium Pansophicum*, I-III. Only when the Will is dually personified as Kāmadeva and Rati can it be said that the Will-spirit and the Craving are actually distinguished: elsewhere, either *kāma* represents the Will as an undivided principle, or we must understand from the context *what* will is implied. In our text, especially vv. 1 and 4, where it is Death, Privation, Godhead, that wills (*syām*, *akāmayat*)—a thing that can only be conceived analogically in the Not-Self—we must understand it is not the Will-spirit (*kāma*, *libido*, "lubet"), but the Craving (*tṛṣṇa*, coveting, fatality, that which "draws a man on" when he is "fey"); that is the desire of Nature (*prakṛti*) for intrinsic form (*svarūpa*), the ardour of the Waters "in their season," *Pañcaviṁśa Brāhmaṇa*, VII, 8, 1, an unconscious, functional, dark will-to-life. In X, 129, 4 (p. 55) on the other hand, where *kāma* is identified with the "primal seed (*retas*) of Intellect (*manas*)"—not, i.e., the germinal *source* of Intellect, but the germinal *aspect* of Intellect, *logos spermatikos*, the *rasa* of *Ṛg Veda*, I, 164, 8—the light Will-spirit is clearly implied. The two wills are immediately correlated and perfectly balanced in unitary being: representing His knowledge of himself (in both senses of the verb to "know"). In other words, the movement of the Will-spirit towards its object is the "answer" to the unspoken "wish" of the unconscious, as in *Ṛg Veda*, I, 164, 8, "He by Intellect forewent her." These considerations seem to solve the difficulties felt by Keith, *Religion and Philosophy of the Veda*, p. 436.

15 *Ṛg Veda*, VII, 33, 11, *Bṛhad Devatā*, V, 148 and 149, and *Sarvānukramaṇī*, I, 166: the child begotten of Mitra-Varuṇau and the Waters is Vasiṣṭha, who like Brahmā makes his appearance upon a lotus, i.e., is established in the Waters, in the possibility of existence, and who is in fact the same as Brahmā-Prajāpati, as rightly identified in the *Śatapatha Brāhmaṇa*, II, 4, 4, 2, cf. *Nirukta*, V, 14. Hence Vasiṣṭha's patronymic Maitrā-varuṇi. Again in the *Aitareya Āraṇyaka*, II, 2, 1 and 2, Vasiṣṭha and other "sages" are identified in various ways with the progenitive Person and the positive existence of all things. In *Atharva Veda*, X, 8, 20, the expression "churned forth" (*nirmanthate*), appropriate to Agni, is used of Vasu (= Vasiṣṭha). The name Vasiṣṭha (superlative of *vasu*) seems to be rightly understood by the Commentators to mean "foremost of those who dwell, exist, or live," either from root *vas* "to assume a form," or root *vas* "to live," or "abide in a given condition." *Vasu* is also derivable from root *vas* to shine, giving the secondary meaning "wealth." Whatever the root, the meanings are not incompatible, inasmuch as to be unindigent of life or existence is the primary "good." Cf. Vasudhā, Vasudharā, Earth as "Mistress of Wealth," "Habundia," or "Upbearer of Life" (Vasudhā also = Lakṣmī); and Vasudhara, Kṛṣṇa as "Lord of Life" in relation to Rādhā, where both meanings are implied.

Like Vasiṣṭha, Agni (Vaiśvānara) is born of, literally "churned from" a lotus, i.e., the Earth, *Ṛg Veda*, VI, 16, 13. That is, as the element of Fire and as Sacrificial Fire in the Three Worlds: for Agni as the Supreme Deity is the "Father," being like Mitra-Varuṇa seduced by the Waters, *Taittirīya Brāhmaṇa*, I, 1, 3, 8, and *Śatapatha Brāhmaṇa*, II, 1, 1, 4 and 5. Needless to point out that Mitra-Varuṇa, Sun, Fire, Spirit, etc., are all denotations of one and the same first principle of manifestation, and that the Waters, often called the wives of Varuṇa, or mothers in relation to the Son (Kumāra, Agni Vaiśvānara), are the possibilities of manifestation.

Parallel to the passages cited above is the myth of Purūravas and Urvaśī, *Ṛg Veda*, X, 95 (also IV, 2, 12 and 18), and *Śatapatha Brāhmaṇa*, XI, 5, 1; their son Āyu, "Life," is identified in the *Vājasaneyī Saṁhitā*, V, 2, with Agni, Fire. Purūravas evidently corresponds to Prajāpati, the "first sacrificer," cf. how in the ŚBr. passage he brings fire to earth by performing the (first) sacrifice, that is after he has lain again with Urvaśī on "the last night of the year" subsequent to their first intercourse, that means a year of supernal time, the duration of one cycle of manifestation, the "Year" of our Upaniṣad. By the sacrifice, he who had been "changed in form" and "walked amongst mortals," and was thus divided from Urvaśī (manifestation, or existence necessarily implying a diremption of essence and nature) he becomes a Gandharva, and is reunited with Urvaśī, that is he becomes again the pure Will-spirit in union with its object. Thus he has proceeded in time, and now returns to the unmanifest at the end of time. Thus also Purūravas corresponds to Āditya (Vivasvat): Āyu may be compared to Manu Vaivasvata. The "mortality" of Purūravas does not mean that Purūravas was "a man," but belongs to his existence as Universal Man, *saguṇa*, *martya* Brahman. That all this was clearly understood is shown in connection with the Soma sacrifice, when in the ritual of making fire, the upper and the lower twirling-sticks are addressed as Purūravas and Urvaśī, the pan of *ghī* (the food of the sacrificial fire, whereby it *exists*) as Āyu, "for Urvaśī was the Apsaras, Purūravas her Lord, from their intercourse was Āyu born, and now in like manner he (the sacrificer) brings forth the sacrifice from their union," *Śatapatha Brāhmaṇa*, III, 4, 1, 22.

The relations between Vivasvant (the mortal Sun) and Saraṇyū (in person or represented by a *savarṇā*) are the same as those of Purūravas and Urvaśī: Āyu corresponding to Yama-Yamī, Manu, and the Aśvins.

It may be added that *-ravas* in Pururavas, and Ravi, "Sun," are from the same *√ru*, to "roar"; the notion being that of the roaring of the Cosmic Fire (*Ṛg Veda*, V, 2, 10), which is the purring of the World-Wheel, the Music of the Spheres. Cf. *Maitri Up.*, II,, 6 (*c*).

Note that the designation of the upper fire-stick, *pramantha*, corresponds to "Prometheus." The correspondence between the myths of Purūravas and Urvaśī and Eros and Psyche is evident. Prometheus is post-Homeric, the myth of Eros and Psyche only in Apuleius: *pra-√math* occurs first in Smṛti, corresponding to *nir-√math* in Vedic usage. The importance of Fire and Water in early Greek philosophy may well reflect Oriental, that is immediately, Persian influences, cf. Harrison, *Themis*, 1927, p. 461. It may be noted that the correspondence of Prometheus with *pramantha* is far more than merely etymological. Prometheus, like Agni, is the child of Earth, and the Okeanids who sympathise with him (in the Prometheus of Aeschylus) are his blood-kin, for the birth of Fire on Earth is but one remove from his source in the Waters. Like Urvaśī, these Okeanids appear to him in the form of birds; and "Okeanos is much more than Ocean."

As for the diremption of essence and nature (represented in our myths by Purūravas and Urvaśī, Eros and Psyche), cf. *Taittirīya Brāhmaṇa*, I, 1, 3, 2, "The sky and earth were close together. On being divided, they said, etc.," with the famous fragment of Euripides (Nauck, frg. 484): Cf. RV. I, 164, 8–9, X, 124, 8 and JUB. III, 14.)

Heaven and Earth were once one form, but stirred
And strove and dwelt asunder far away:
And then rewedding, bore unto the day
And light of life all things that are . . .
. . . each in his kind and law,

and the later echo in *Apollonius Rhodius*, I, 494, " how that they parted after deadly strife asunder, etc."

For a comparative treatment of the whole theme see Siecke, E., *Die Liebesgeschichte des Himmels*, Strassburg, 1892.

Amongst the proposed derivations of *apsaras*, that which gives the sense " moving on the Waters " is to be preferred, but *apsu-rasa*, " savour of the Waters " is also possible, and a third derivation from *a-psā*, implying " forbidden food," also suggested by Yāska, is not without interest. Vedic Apsaras and Gandharva are a single pair; the former, by name Urvaśī (" wide-pervasive ") is a persona of Aditi, later represented as Śrī-Lakṣmī, the latter equivalent to Kandarpa, Kāmadeva. In any case, the Apsaras represents the fascination of the possibilities of existence, to which the Will, Gandharva, responds: their mutual relation is the *causa causans* of the movement of the world. It is again as Will that the Gandharva holds the bridle of the cosmic steed, i.e., Varuṇa, *Taittirīya Saṁhitā*, IV, 6, 7, and *Ṛg Veda*, I, 163, 3.

Observe that *nirukta* is not " etymology," but " interpretation," 'ερμηνέια. Yāska never had in view the special science of philology, and it is merely " unscientific " to speak of his " derivations " as " false etymologies." Neither is *nirukta* merely " exegesis " (concrete interpretation), but rather " anagogic. Examples of *nairukta*, " hermeneutic," interpretation would be (1) to correlate Grk. προβατικός with Lat. *probare*, in the sense to " prove," " make good," (2) to compare A and ŌM with Alpha and Omega, (3) to explain *amor* as *a-mor* = *amṛta*. At the same time nothing hinders that *nirukta* may in certain cases accord with " true etymology."

16 Or as expressed by Jīlī, while religion (dualism) distinguishes ice (the universe) from water (God), understanding (monism) realises their identity (Nicholson, *Studies* . . . p. 99).

17 Cf. Jīlī's " nine phases of will, beginning with inclination (*mayl*) and ending with the highest and purest love (*'ishq*) in which there is no (distinction of) lover or beloved," Nicholson, *Studies* . . . p. 102.

18 Cf. *Bhagavad Gītā*, II, 12 and XIII, 19; Śaṅkarâcārya, Comment. on the *Vedânta Sūtra*, II, 1, 35, *anāditvātsaṁsārasya*; and Dante, " nor before nor after was the procession of God's outflowing over these waters," but " where every where and every when is focussed," *Paradiso*, XXIX, 13, 20, and 21.

19 Mṛtyu as Death-absolute, the last death of the soul, *mors janua vitae*, is to be distinguished from death-temporal, *mṛtyu*, or *punar mṛtyu*; which distinction is, for example, sharply drawn in the seventh stanza of our brāhmaṇa.

It is developed above, p. 32, that the relation of Godhead to God, *nirguṇa* Brahman (Mṛtyu in our text), is as it were maternal, a relation of Aditi to Āditya. Observe then that corresponding to the conception in our text of *nirguṇa*, *anātmya* Brahman as Death-absolute is that of Aditi as Nirṛti, as in *Ṛg Veda*, VII, 58, 1, where the Maruts rise up, grow up, into the regions of angelhood (*daivasya dhāmnaḥ*) from the abyss of Nirṛti (*nirṛteravaṁśāt*)—the metaphor contrasts *dhāman* in the sense of "abode," "dwelling," having an implied structure, with that which is not an abode, not a dwelling, but without structure, literally "devoid of any beam," *avaṁśa*, and "unsupported by any pillar," *askambha*.

Daivasya dhāman here corresponds to *akṣara . . . dhāma parama*, "imperishable, transcendent abode," *Bhagavad Gītā*, VIII, 21.

20 "The Self is neither this nor that (*neti, neti*): unseizable, indestructible, unrelated, etc.," *Bṛhadāraṇyaka Up.*, IV, 4, 22.

Cf. also Dante, *Convivio*, III, 15, ". . . certain things which our intellect cannot behold . . . we cannot understand what they are except by denying things of them."

The same argument is developed in Maimonides, *Guide for the Perplexed*, I, 59.

21 All this exactly corresponds to the Muḥammadan conception of the Godhead as al'Amā, "dark mist," "blindness," "unconsciousness," immanent negativity," "potentiality," "non-existence," etc., all logically contrasted with Aḥaddiya, the transcendental Unity of Allāh (Nicholson, *Studies* . . . pp. 83-97).

22 Franklin Edgerton, *The Upanisads: what do they teach, and why?* J.A.O.S., 49, pp. 97-121.

23 In full, "Not to have gain of any good unto himself, which may not be, but that his splendour, counter-shining, might declare, 'I am.'" Cf. Plotinus, *Enneads*, V, 3, 8, "a splendour directed to itself, which at one and the same time illuminates, and is itself illuminated."

24 *Arpitam*, "infixed," "projected," geometrically, pictorially, and spatially in the Tree of Life. Cf. Dante's "trina luce, che in unica stella scintillando." *Paradiso*, XXXI, 28: Eckhart, I, 282, "Everything is pictured in his providence." The Son is *viśvarūpa*.

25 Corresponding to all this is the Islamic doctrine or "metaphor of Allāh's creating by looking (*naẓar*)," for "towards everything that Allāh created he has a special aspect (*wajh* = "face"), in virtue of which he regards it and preserves it in its appointed place in the order of existence," see Macdonald, D.B., *Development of the Idea of Spirit in Islam*, Acta Orientalia, IX, 1931, p. 347, and Nicholson, R. A., *Studies in Islamic mysticism*, 1921, p. 110, 114.

26 Cf. also Śaṅkarācārya, *Dakṣiṇāmūrtistotra*, I, *darpaṇa-dṛśyamāna*, "as if reflected in a mirror." Or again, from Jīlī, *Insānu'l kāmil*, Ch. LX, "As a mirror in which a person sees the form of himself and cannot see it without a mirror, such is the relation of God to the Perfect Man, who cannot possibly see his own form but in the mirror of the name Allāh; and he is also a mirror to God, for God laid upon himself the necessity that His names and attributes should not be seen save in the Perfect Man," Nicholson, *Studies* . . . p. 106. Or yet again, Eckhart, "It is as if one stood before a high mountain, and cried, 'Art thou there?' The echo comes back, 'Art thou there?' If one cries, 'Come out,' the echo answers, 'Come out'" (Claud Field's *Eckhart's Sermons*, p. 26): as in the *Chāndogya Up.*, I, 3, 2, *samāna u evāyaṁ cāsau . . . svara itīmam—ācakṣate svara iti pratyāsvara ityamum*, with double entendre, (1) "This is called 'Sound,' That 'Sound,' viz., an 'Echoing,'" and (2) "This is regarded as 'Light,' That 'Light,' viz., 'Reflection.'" It may be observed that the same dual significance is present also in our Upaniṣad, I, 2, 1, translated above, where *arcan acarat* can mean either "lauded with lauds," or "manifested light."

The principle involved underlies and explains the offering of lights and music in devotional offices: that is as it were a re-flection of His light and sound upon Himself, whereby His likeness (*mūrtti*, *pratimā*, or other *pratīka*) is revealed to the officiant, which likewise otherwise remains unseen and uneloquent, alone in its dark shrine.

The metaphor of reflection implies, of course, a correspondence of microcosm and macrocosm, cf. " Yonder world is the counterpart (*anurūpam*) of this world, and of yonder world this world is the counterpart," *Aitareya Brāhmaṇa*, VIII, 2.

[27] Cf. Böhme, " even thy own earth also (that is, thy body)," *Supersensual Life*; Sāyaṇa, on *Ṛg Veda*, VI, 16, 13, *bhūmiśca sarvajagat-ādhāra-bhūt'ti*, " Earth is the support of every world "; and *Bṛhadāraṇyaka Up.*, II, 5, 1, " This Earth is honey for all creatures," i.e., the support of their existence, each after its kind.

In *Ṛg Veda*, I, 108, 9, and X, 59, 4, respectively, the Three Worlds, and Heaven and Earth, are spoken of as " Earths."

[28] The root *tap* can also be employed transitively, as in *Aitareya Āraṇyaka*, II, 4, where *ātmā . . . puruṣam . . . abhyatapat*, where *abhyatapat* has been rendered by Max Müller and others as " brooded upon," no doubt with reference to the idea of a brooding hen. Something like the transformation of energy into heat by an interposition of resistance is involved. With *tapas* may be compared not only Hebrew *zimzum*, but also German *sude* as used by Böhme, and explained by Law as "a boiling or seething . . . the stirring of the seven properties in nature."

[29] In Christian art the Tree of Jesse corresponds to the Vedic descriptions of the Tree of Life (*Ṛg Veda*, I, 24, 7, *Atharva Veda*, X, 7, 38, *Kaṭha Up.*, and *Maitri Up.*, as cited here), and to the later representations of the Birth of Brahmā. See my *Tree of Jesse*, Art Bulletin, XI, 2, 1929, and *Yakṣas*, II, 1931, also Strzygowski, *Asiatische Miniaturmalerei*, 1932, p. 167.

[30] Not infrequently, e.g., in *Bṛhad Devatā*, I, 69, " Indra and Vāyu " are counted as one Person in this Trinity. On Indra, see p. 73f.

It must, of course, be understood that Vedic " theology " takes account of two different kinds of Trinity, (1) ontological, analogous to the Christian concept, and (2) that of the Trimūrti of Persons distinguished functionally. Both are " arrangements " of One Power, but made from different points of view. The Universe is three-fold from many distinct points of view.

[31] It will be realised, of course, that Āditya, the Supernal-Sun, Child of Aditi, Petrarch's *il somme sol*, Dante's *somma luce*, is not merely our sidereal sun, but shines as the first principle of Light and Time throughout the " hundred years " of the lifetime of Brahmā-Prajāpati, the one " year " of our Upaniṣad. The Supernal-Sun is the " Father of Lights " in the Three Worlds. " As the Deity, viz., the divine light, is the centre of all life, so also in the manifestation of God, viz., in the figure (i.e., *pratīka*), the sun is the centre of all life," Böhme, *Signatura Rerum*, IV, 18, cf. *Maitri Up.*, VI, 30. As Swedenborg expresses it, " it is evident that in the spiritual world there is a different sun from that of the natural world."

[32] Our rendering of *nirvāṇa, nirvāta*, as " despiration," etc., is based on etymological grounds, cf., *avāta*, " without spiration " and on the fundamental connotation. But it should not be overlooked that in later and especially Buddhist usage it is an extinction rather of the flame

than of the breath of life that is immediately denoted. The distinction rather logical than real; *kāma* and *prāṇa* being inseparable "movements," simultaneous alike in origination and cessation. "Deflagration" might have been a better rendering of (Buddhist) *nirvāṇa*, but the use in Physics of deflagration as practically equivalent to conflagration makes this difficult. The to be preferred renderings of Buddhist *nirvāṇa* and *parinirvāṇa* seem to be "Extinction" and "Total Extinction," with reference, that is, to the *flame* of life.

[33] "Prajāpati" occurs in the *Ṛg Veda*, viz., IV, 53, 2, as an epithet of Savitṛ as Universal Mover, and X, 121, 10, again as an epithet of the Supernal-Sun.

[34] *Ṛg Veda*, X, 168, 4, *ātmā devānām, bhuvanasya garbha*.
Cf. *Jaiminīya Brāhmaṇa*, II, 77, "Who is the one and only Angel? Spirit (*prāṇa*)," and *Jaiminīya Upaniṣad Brāhmaṇa*, III, 1, 1, "There is but one entire Angel (viz. Vāyu), the others are but semi-Angels."

[35] For Vāyu as the dawn-wind of creation see especially *Ṛg Veda*, I, 134, where it is clear that the wind is thought of as precedent to dawn, being indeed called upon to awaken the dawn. It may be added that "Dawn" (Uṣas, etc.) in the Vedic hymns generally refers to dawn of a cycle of manifestation, not merely any dawn (human dawns are but in the analogy of cosmic dawns, just as human years are but analogies of supernal "years").

[36] As expressed by Śaṅkarācārya, "His nature is inscrutable," *na ca svabhāvaḥ paryanuyoktum śakyate*, Comment on Brahma Sūtra, I, 2, 33.

[37] Blake's "Man is born like a garden, ready planted and sown": Jung, "The psychological individual . . . has an *a priori* unconscious existence," *Psychological types*, p. 560.
Böhme's conception of the one harmony and its necessarily diverse manifestations has its equivalent in the theology of Jīlī, where every divine "attribute has its effect (*āthār*) in which its *jamāl* or *jalāl* or *kamāl* is manifested" so that "Paradise is the mirror of absolute *jamāl*, Hell of absolute *jalāl*," Nicholson, *Studies* . . . p. 100.

[37a] The primordial causality of intrinsic nature (*svabhāva*) is categorically denied in *Śvetāśvatara Up.*, I, 2 and VI, 1. The contradiction involved is more apparent than real, and depends on the distinction of "cause" from "means." It is indeed "by the Allmight of the Angel (i.e., the "Father") that this Brahma-wheel revolves"; but the position of each existent (*sthita* = *avyāpaka*) thing, its specific modality, is determined by qualities inherent in the thing itself.
This intrinsic nature, whereby each thing is what it is, constitutes the private measure of free will of each thing, though its autonomy is limited by the coexistence of other things.
The question, whether God as he is in himself knows good and evil as we know them can be answered with assurance in the negative by the consideration that He cannot be thought of as subjected to limitations of individuality; the knowledge of good and evil belongs to *avidyā*, "ignorance," "relativity." In the same way with respect to causal operation, a temporal separation of cause and effect being inconceivable from the standpoint of absolute understanding (*vidyā*). Cf. *Ṛg. Veda*, I, 164, 32, "He who hath made him (Agni Vaiśvānara) knows him not."
It may be noted that *Genesis*, III, 22, now translated "The Lord God said, Behold the man is become as one of us to know good and evil," should have been rendered "Behold the man who hath been like one

of us, is come to know good through evil," cf. Ogden and Richards, *The Meaning of meaning*, 3rd. ed. 1930, p. 224, Note 1, and cf. also our Note 109 *infra*.

[38] In case the doctrine of reincarnation was originally of popular origin, this would mean "first intellectual formulation": whenever that may have been. Liberation and rebirth are already distinguished and contrasted in Ṛg Veda, V, 46, I, in the phrase *vimucaṁ na āvṛttam punaḥ* "neither liberation nor coming back again."

[39] This Law, of which the ordinances (*dharmāṇi*) are established by the first sacrifice, *Ṛg Veda*, X, 90, 16, might be stated as follows: Within the realm of causality, causality operates uniformly, through time and time again. Moreover, as the creation (sacrifice) is without beginning or end, so also is the Law without beginning or end.

[40] Eckhart, I, 379, "Aught is suspended from the divine essence; its progression is matter, wherein the soul puts on new forms and puts off her old ones. The change from one into the other is her death: the one she doffs she dies to, and the one she dons she lives in," presents a remarkable likeness to *Bhagavad Gītā*, II, 22, "As a man casting off worn-out garments, taketh other new ones, so the embodied being, casting off worn out bodies, enters into other new ones." I do not infer that Eckhart is speaking of re-incarnation, in the accepted sense of the word, but rather that he is referring to a progress in wisdom of the individual Self, as in the *Bṛhadāraṇyaka Up.*, IV, 4, 4, "just so this Self, striking down this body and driving out its ignorance, makes for itself another newer and fairer form, such as that of the Patriarchs, Choristers, Angels, Prajāpati, Brahmā, or other living beings." Both this passage, and that cited from the *Gītā* could be, and perhaps should be understood to mean not a reincarnation of the individual, but the continuous reincarnation of the Spirit, in forms causally determined by past acts, and so inherited by other, not the same, individuals. Just as we invoke such names as gene or germ-plasm to account for character and species.

[41] So there is a *daivya parimara* = Götterdämmerung, *Kauṣītaki Up.*, I, 12.

[42] That "insofar" is doctrinally an important point. For pantheism and "natural religion" are excluded equally by the Vedas and in Christianity. Primarily, in that infinity is incommensurable with the totality of things finite. Also explicitly, "Only one-fourth of him is born here," *Ṛg Veda*, X, 90, 4; "Heaven and Earth have not measured, nor do they measure, his omnipotence" *ibid.*, III, 82, 37; "Thou dost insist beyond all things, the several worlds," *ibid.*, I, 81, 5 and I, 102, 8; "of the bright power that pervades the sky it is but a part," *Maitri Up.*, VI, 35; "not I in them, but they in Me," *na tvahaṁ teṣu te mayi*, *Bhagavad Gītā*, VII, 12, "I am existent only in a fraction," *aham . . . ekāṁśena sthitaḥ*, *ibid.*, X, 42. "God enjoys himself in all things . . . yet he loses nothing of his brightness," Eckhart, I, 143; "of that also is the creation, but not in the omnipotence and power, but like an apple which grows upon the tree, which is not the tree itself, but grows from the power of the tree," Böhme, *Signatura Rerum*, XVI, 1; "See now the height and breadth of the eternal Worth, which hath made for itself so many mirrors wherein it is refracted, and yet remains within itself One, as before," Dante, *Paradiso*, XXIX, 142-145.

In general, the notion of "pantheism," read into any doctrine, arises from a confusion of the unity which is one in itself, with the merely collective totality of all things.

[43] " All evils and afflictions as well as all kinds of happiness of man . . . are distributed according to justice," Maimonides, *Guide for the Perplexed*, III, 17. To be merciful is to be unjust : " have the seasons, gravitation, the appointed days, mercy ? no more have I," Whitman, *Chanting the Square Deific*.

[44] That Self-intention is his knowledge of him-Self, as it were a *maithuna*, carnal knowledge, of Wisdom, *vāc* : the " cause " of the becoming of the world, for what is " concept " therein is a thing begotten and proceeding, after the way of things " conceived."

[45] Śaṅkarâcārya, *Svâtmanirūpaṇa*, 95. The concept of a world-picture is implicit in *Ṛg Veda*, I, 164, 44, *viśvam abhicaṣṭe*.

[46] Cf. also Jīlī, as cited by Nicholson, *Studies* . . . p. 113 : " Allāh created Adam in his own image . . . and Adam was one of the theatres in which I displayed myself," and *ibid.*, 108, " I am that whole, and the whole is my theatre." On Indian *līlā* see Śaṅkarâcārya on *Vedânta Sūtra*, II, 1, 33.

[47] The " articulation " (a + u + m) of the Imperishable-Word, OṀ, should be observed. See Note 109 : cf. also Bhagavan Dās, *The science of peace*, 1904.

[48] *Apara* is often understood to mean " western," but is here assuredly used in its primary sense, that is just as when we speak of *para* and *apara* Brahman. For the upper and the nether Waters in Indian tradition see, e.g., *Ṛg Veda*, III, 22, 3, and *Taittirīya Saṁhitā*, IV, 2, 4, where the Waters of the Sun are spoken of as *parastāt*, and those below are *avastāt* (= *aparastāt* or *apara*) : and *Ṛg Veda*, X, 136, 5, where the two seas are *pūrva* and *apara*, commonly understood to mean eastern and western. Not forgetting that these are cosmic seas, of which the Bay of Bengal and the Arabian sea are merely symbols, it is quite intelligible that upper and nether should have been taken alternatively to mean eastern and western : for just as the sidereal sun rises in an actual East and sets in an actual West, so must the Supernal-Sun rise in analogically " eastern " and set in analogically " western " waters.

Both seas were originally Varuṇa's (cf. p. 33). Why then is Varuṇa later particularly connected with the West, the night, the Moon, and not always with the East *and* West, the Sun *and* Moon, the day and night ? Because the dual Mitra-Varuṇau had been originally the personal name of manifested deity conceived under two aspects, viz., as Varuṇa "at birth" (*jāyase*) and as Mitra "when enkindled " (*samiddhvaḥ*), *Ṛg Veda*, V, 3, 1, and III, 5, 4 : " at birth," that would be as the Fiery-Energy (*tejas*, *mahi*) of intension (*tapas*), cf. *Ṛg Veda*, *X*, 129, 2, *tapasaḥ*, *mahinā ajāvat* ; " when enkindled," that would be in procession as Light (*prakāśa*) manifested by the dark-heat (*uṣṇa*), *Maitri Up.*, VII, 11, *samīraṇe prakāśa-prakṣepauṣṇyasthānīya*. In the dual Mitra-Varuṇau, Mitra, " the Friend," designates the terrestrial Agni, so often spoken of in the same way as the " Friend " of man, this terrestrial Agni being the Son or manifested form of Varuṇa himself ; as in the one hymn devoted solely to Mitra, he is the Mouthpiece (*bruvāṇaḥ*), the all-seeing Eye in the world (*animiṣā abhicaṣṭe*, cf. the Buddha as *cakkhuṁ loke*, *Dīgha Nikāya*, II, 158), the common denominator of all men in that he " unites " (*yātayati*) them, and who upholds (*dadhāra*, *askambhayat*) heaven and earth. That Mitra is commonly thought of as a celestial aspect, viz., solar, as also in the Avesta, though described as terrestrial in *Ṛg Veda*, III, 59, presents no difficulty ; for Agni's dual birth (*dvijanma*) is in heaven and on earth (*dyāvā-pṛthivīya*), both on high and here below, the two fires are "one Angel" as in our text (see p. 37); just as in Christian phraseology, "I and my Father are One," Son being also Sun (see p. 43 and cf. Notes 10 and 48).

49 In this sense the whole ritual may be regarded as "Mysterium und Mimus," and the question whether or not any particular Vedic hymn should be regarded as "dramatic" loses its significance.

50 "This eternal Brahman is at once the Imperishable-Word (*akṣara*) and the Word-that-can-be-spoken (*vācya*)," *Bṛhad Devatā*, I, 62. Utterance (*vyāhṛti*) is further discussed below, Note 62. *Bhān* = Fiat Lux.

51 I.e., what could be called in Greek the "Eniautos-Daimon."

52 For Buddhism, and the doctrine of the identity of all teaching, see particularly the *Saddharma Puṇḍarīka*. In all but name the Tathāgata is identified with Brahmā-Prajāpati.

53 Likewise no more and no less "demiurge" than is the "Perfect Man" (*al-insānu'l kāmil*) of Islamic theology, viz., Allāh's Word or Fiat (*amr*) and Spirit (*rūḥ*) manifested in the transcendental being of the Prophet (Muḥammad) as the principle and archetype of all existences.

54 "Good, pious souls, are hindered too from their proper object by lingering with holy joy over the human form of our Lord Jesus Christ.... To them his manhood is a hindrance so long as they cling to it with mortal pleasure; they ought to follow God in all his ways and not keep solely to his way of manhood who reveals to us the way of Godhood," Eckhart, I, 187.

54a On the significance of the begetting of a son, see *Aitareya Brāhmaṇa*, VII, 13 (*HOS*., Vol. 25, pp. 299, 300).

55 For example, "God's speaking is his child-bearing," St. Augustine; "The Word proceeding is properly called begotten and Son . . . conception and birth," St. Thomas, *Sum. Th.*, I, Q. 27, A. 2. *Solus ante principium* = *pūrṇa apravartin, Kauṣītaki Up.*, IV, 5.

56 Also *Bṛhadāraṇyaka Up.*, I, 4, 17, *prāṇa prajā*; and *Taittirīya Up.*, I, 3, 3.

To render *vāc* consistently by one and the same English word would be impossible. A distinction of *Vāc*, synonymous with Sarasvatī in *Ṛg Veda*, I, 3, 12, and representing an aspect of Māyā, Prakṛti, Śakti, Omnipotentia, from *vāc*, "word" or "language" must be clearly recognized. In the beginning, as conjoint principle with Intellect, *Vāc* is Sophia, Dante's "Wisdom": "in highest praise of Wisdom, I say that she is the mother of all first principles, affirming that she was with God when in the beginning he made the world, and specially the movement of the heaven which engenders all things, whereby every other movement is originated and set going; adding, 'she was the thought of Him who set the universe in motion'; I mean that she was in the divine thought, which is very intellect, when He made the world. Whence it follows that she made it; and therefore Solomon on the book of *Proverbs* says speaking in the person of Wisdom, 'When God prepared the heavens, I was there, when he fenced the depths with a fixed law and a fixed circle, when He set fast the firmament above, when He hung aloft the fountains of the waters, when he encircled the sea with its boundary, and laid down a decree for the waters that they should not pass their borders, when he laid the foundations of the earth, I was with Him disposing all things, and I took my pleasure every day,'" *Convivio*, III, 15; cf. *Ṛg Veda*, X, 71 and X, 95.

57 Jīlī, on Qur'ān, II, 14, 23 f., cited by Nicholson, *Studies* . . . p. 113.

58 For Heraclitus (who was regarded by St. Justin as a "Christian before Christ") the Logos, manifesting as Fire, is that universal principle which animates and rules the world. This non-dualistic point of view is more fully developed by the Stoics, in a fashion again suggesting Indian contacts: according to them "God did not make the world as an artisan does his work, but it is by wholly penetrating all matter that He is the demiurge of the universe (Galen, *De qual. incorp.* in *Fr. Stoic.* ed. von Arnim, II, 6); He penetrates the world 'as honey does the honeycomb' (Tertullian, *Adv. Hermogenem*, 44); this God so intimately mingled with the world is fire or ignited air; inasmuch as He is the principle controlling the universe, He is called *Logos*; and inasmuch as He is the germ from which all else develops, He is called the *seminal Logos* (*Logos spermatikos*). This Logos is at the same time a force and a law, an irresistible force which bears along the entire world and all creatures to a common end, an inevitable and holy law from which nothing can withdraw itself, and which every reasonable man should follow willingly' (Cleanthus, *Hymn to Zeus* in *Fr. Stoic.*, I, 527—cf. 537). Conformably to their exegetical habits the Stoics made of the different gods personifications of the Logos, e.g., of Zeus, and above all of Hermes," *Catholic Encyclopedia, s.v. Logos.*

The correspondence and probable connection of this ideology with that of the Upaniṣads is obvious. The more special application of Cleanthus may be likened to the Buddhist concept of *dharma-cakra pravartana*.

59 Eckhart speaks of the "maternal names" of God in two different senses: when he calls him the "Mother of all things," that is not in the present sense of "natural parent," but in that "he stays with all creatures to keep them in being," I, 1427. That would be in Indian terms, in his Person as Viṣṇu, or as in our text, 7, where he "remembers" (*manyata*) all existences for as long as time endures: that in scientific phraseology is the "conservation of energy," cf. Note 75.

60 Kāla, our "Father Time," but here essentially, not as now merely allegorically.

61 Represented in the later iconography by the demons Madhu and Kaiṭabha, threatening Brahmā, lotus-seated and navel-born from Nārâyaṇa.

62 Utterance, *vyāhṛti*, is that of the Three Worlds, as explained in the *Maitri Up.*, VI, 6; these worlds, this universe, being the body (*tanu, śarīra*) of Prajāpati, the Horse, the Tree, the Wheel, the Dance of Śiva.

The analysis of the singular name or utterance into its manifold aspects is the co-creative function of the poetic genius, imagination, or prophecy, expressed primarily in the sacrificial chants. Cf. "When, O Bṛhaspati, calling things by their names (Prophets), put forth the head and front of Wisdom (*vāc*), then what was best and flawless in them, hid in the innermost (*guhā*), that by their love (*preman*) they brought to light . . . by Intellect (*manas*) they dealt with Wisdom (*vāc*)," hence it is said that "by the Sacrifice they found the tracks of Wisdom, within the Prophets (*ṛṣi*) lodged," *Rg Veda*, X, 71, 3: for "Whom I (viz., Wisdom, *vāc*) love, him I make forceful, Brahman, Prophet, and very wise," *ibid.*, X, 125, 5. Access to this unspoken Wisdom in the innermost, is spoken of as vision and audition (—*dṛś* and —*śru*), *ibid.*, X, 71, 4, hence the later designation of the Veda as *śruti*, "that which was heard."

63 *Sṛṣṭi*, *asṛjata*, *asṛgram*, etc., ought not to be translated as "crea-

tion" and "created." For though *sṛj* may denote the same as *kṛ*, the connotation is quite different, in the first case to "pour out," "emanate," in the second to "make," "create," "fashion." Thus *sṛj* and *kṛ* are the terms proper respectively to metaphysical, and to dualistic parlance, and they should not be confused in translation. For *sṛṣṭi*, etc., English "emanated," "outpoured," "outflown," etc., are immediately available.

The root *kṣar* in the transitive sense of to "pour-forth" is similarly employed in connection with the notion of Utterance (*vyāhṛti*), *Aitareya Āraṇyaka*, II, 2, 2: in that he pours-forth (*kṣarati*) gifts, and none can exceed this his generosity, a syllable is "*akṣara*." Or *kṣar* being intransitively in the sense of to "flow away," or "perish," *akṣara* means "imperishable," and especially "the Imperishable-Word," OṀ. "Creation," in other words, is fontal, its flux is never diminished: the plenitude (*pūrṇa, bhūman*) of the unity-of-potentiality-and-act is infinite, "The yon is all, and this is all, take all from all from, withdrawing all from all, still over and above remains the all," *Śatapatha Brāhmaṇa*, XIV, 8, 1 = *Bṛhadāraṇyaka Up.*, V, 1; cf. *Atharva Veda*, X, 8, 29.

Nor should *bhūta*, literally "that which has come into existence," although equivalent to Christian "creature," be so translated, nor even as "being"; for in the first place, existences are generally spoken of in Vedic texts as "emanated," rather than as "created," and in the second, while it is true that all existences have being, not all being has existence. A common equivalent of *bhūta* as "an existence" is *sattva*, cf. below, pp. 102-103. *Bhū* = werden, *sthā* = *exstare*.

64 Here "Principles" seems to convey the sense rather better than "Intellect," though both amount to the same thing. We take for granted the definition, "Intellect is the habit of First Principles," and Eckhart, I, 74, "Intellect is a matter of pure being." Will and Intellect the gateway (*mukha, dvāra*) of procession (*prasaraṇa*).

65 Here some further light can be thrown upon the terms corresponding to East and West, Upper and Nether, discussed above, p. 86, Note 48. In the epic account of the Churning of the Ocean, the stallion Uccaiḥśravas, the same as our Cosmic Horse, is called Vaḍabā-bhartri, "the Mare's Husband"; cf. the Vedic myth of Saraṇyū = Apyā, upon whom the Sun (Vivasvant) in the form of a stallion begets the Aśvins (*Ṛg Veda*, X, 13, 4, etc., see Bloomfield in *J.A.O.S.*, Vol. 15, pp. 172 ff.). It follows that the Mare's mouth (*vaḍabāmukha*) and Fire beneath the Waters at the southern pole (Nadir) must correspond to the Stallion's fiery mouth in our Upaniṣad, I, 1, 1, and I, 2, 3. In the first of these passages his front (*pūrva*) part is *udya*, his rear (*apara*) part *nimlocan*, in the second the head is *prācī*, the tail *pratīcī*. The correspondence of *pūrva* and *prācī*, and the equivalence of their various meanings in other contexts, will not be overlooked. In *Ṛg Veda*, X, 72, 9, *pūrva* is beyond doubt "above," as well as "primordial" and "ancient," or even "eternal." Any term representing the antithesis to *apara* should, further, be equivalent to "*para*." *Udya* and *nimlocan* indeed imply the places of the rising and setting of the Sun, and so with respect to terrestrial conditions may rightly be rendered as "East" and "West." But it is clear from the correspondences tabulated above, and in the previous note, that the Supernal-Sun Āditya, is thought of as "rising" by the Zenith, and "setting" in the Nadir, as indeed would be required in doctrine of "light and reflection," *prakāsa-vimarṣa*, as in *Kauṣītaki Up.*, IV, 2,

āditye mahat . . . ādarśe pratirūpah, and as discussed on p. 8. It follows that all our terms denoting East and West *here*, mean Upper and Nether *there*. *Uttara* is the superlative of *ud*, "up."

It also follows that *uttara* and *dakṣiṇa*, respectively "northern" and "southern" *here* stand for "Upper," and "Nether" *there*. For as the Mare's mouth" is *dakṣiṇa*, the Stallion's mouth must be *uttara*. That not only throws light on the use of these terms in connection with the *devayāna* and *pitṛyāna*, but shows that *uttara yuga* in *Ṛg Veda*, X, 72, 1 = *pūrva yuga*, *ibid.*, 9, and that both imply the *parama vyoman*, super-celestial Empyrean. Similarly in the *Ṛg Veda*, X, 90, 5, *paścād purah* is both "from East to West," and "from Zenith to Nadir": His body necessarily extends from the Upper to the Nether Waters, for all existence is contained in the intervening-space (*antarikṣa*), and we have already deduced that his head is above, and that also appears in that his eye is the Supernal-Sun.

Pūrva, by contrast with *apūrva*, "latent," has also the sense of "immediate," that is "within you," cf. *brahmaṁ nihitam guhāyaṁ parame vyoman*, *Taittirīya Up.*, II, 1, cf. "when I say the highest I mean the innermost," Eckhart, I, 164. So Dakṣiṇamūrti, "He whose aspect is turned southward," and is therefore thought of as looking from the north, implies also "He who looks from above downwards" and "He who looks from within outwards." Cf. also *Muṇḍaka Up.*, II, 2, 21, where again "west to east" and "south to north" are the same as "below to above;" and *Atharva Veda*, VIII, 9, 8, *paścāt*, "from within."

All this is in fact far more a psychology of space than a cosmology: from Upper to Nether is from the Within to the Without, from knowing subject to known object, from the centre to the felly of the World-wheel. The "back" or "surface" of the Waters must not be understood too literally to mean an actually horizontal or anywise oriented plane, for the Waters are all the possibilities of existence on any plane, pervading measureless space in the lotus of the heart. Proof positive that the "cosmology" is a psychology can be found in the *Chāndogya Up.*, III, 10-11, where it becomes entirely a question of one's spiritual condition whether the sun rises in the East, South, West, or North, until for the Sādhyas it rises in the Zenith and sets in the Nadir, and finally "for those who know the essential-truth (*upaniṣad*) of Brahman, the Supernal-Sun, risen in the Zenith, stands there in the middle, neither setting nor rising (*na nimloca nôdiyāya*), but evermore high-noon (*sakṛd divā*)," and *ibid.*, VIII, 4, 2, "ever illumined (*sakṛd vibhataḥ*) is this Brahma world." Precisely the same point of view is indicated in the *Aitareya Brāhmaṇa*, III, 44, "indeed he never sets, union with him and identity of form and world he attains who knows thus." Cf. Eckhart, I, 86, "the soul mounts up in this light into space, to the zenith at high noon," the morning light being God, the evening light the light of Nature, and noon the light of their identity: Ruysbroeck, "When Christ, the Divine Sun, has risen to the zenith of our hearts . . . then . . . He will draw all things to Himself." Just as also in Islamic theology, the eye (*hamm*) of the heart (*qalb* = *hṛd*) is variously oriented in men of different spiritual degree, but the heart of the Comprehensor has no face or back, "these men face with their whole being the whole of the Divine names and attributes and are with God *essentially*," Nicholson, *Studies* . . . p. 114, Note 3. Cf. Böhme, *Signatura Rerum*, VII, 38, "Now wilt thou be a magus? Then thou must understand how to change the night again into day."

On the other hand, what is called the "ordinary view" of the

Brāhmaṇas, viz., that the Sun is born of the Fire, and sets in the Fire, e.g., *Aitareya Brāhmaṇa*, VIII, 28, refers to the Procession and Recession of the Supernal-Sun as one of the Several Angels of the Trinity, as in *Bṛhadāraṇyaka Up.*, I, 2, 2, and 3. Again in *Ṛg Veda*, I, 35, 3, where Savitṛ moves "by the height and by the depth" (*pravatā, utyavatā*), coming "hither from afar" (*duritā*), illuminating not merely the earth but all the worlds, and is called the axis of the wheel whereby the angels are supported, it is certainly not the physical Sun that is intended, but the Supernal-Sun "whose paths are twain, an inner and an outer," as in *Maitri Up.*, VI, 1, translated below. All these risings and settings take place *antarbhūtasya khe, hṛdayākāśe*, i.e., "within you," "in the heart-space," that is at the same time in the Waters, in the Sea (*Ṛg Veda*, IV, 58 1, *samudre hṛdi*, cf. *Chāndogya Up.*, VIII, 1, 3, "everything here is contained within it"); and endeavours (e.g., Speyers in J.R.A.S., 1906, 723 f.) to interpret "scientifically" are beside the mark: the "science" here is not astronomical, but psychological and ontological. Nothing can be *less* scientific than to assume for Vedic liturgists an interest in natural facts of the same kind as our own. One might as well attempt to explain the stylistic sequences of Asiatic art in terms of a more or less accurate "observation of Nature."

A precisely analogous problem is presented in Chinese "cosmology," cf. Saussure, L. de, *La série septénaire, cosmologique et planétaire*, Journ. Asiatique, XXIV, 1924, pp. 333 f., esp. p. 335, "Le levant et l'occident représentent ainsi la naissance et la mort, le *yang* et le *yin*, comme le font également le sud et le nord." With the "cosmology" of *Chāndogya Up.*, III, 1-11, cf. Lü Tzü's "Circulation of the Light . . . according to its own law" (Wilhelm and Jung, *Secret of the Golden Flower*, p. 57). Here, just as in India, a metaphysical symbolism is based on both the diurnal and the annual movements of the sun, but with this difference that in China the north corresponds to nature, the south to essence. See also the Appendix.

66 Thus no "strange fate" has here "overtaken the Upanishadic Brahman," as Professor Edgerton believed, *The Bhagavad Gita*, 1925, p. 53.

67 With respect to *para* and *apara*, and their equivalents, see p. 86 above. In our Upaniṣad, I, 1, 2, each of the twin Waters, *pūrva* and *apara samudrau*, is spoken of as an "omnipotence," *mahimā* (f.), a very close parallel to Eckhart's "wherefore he is omnipotent," I, 371, cited above. That by no means excludes the interpretation of *mahimā*, also as "sacrificial vessel," cf. the double significance of *dhiṣaṇā*, often in the dual *dhiṣaṇe*; for which see Johansson's admirable pamphlet, *Die altindische Göttin Dhiṣaṇā und Verwandtes*, Uppsala, 1910. Cf. *Ṛg Veda*, III, 45, 3, "Even as deep waters, even as kine, thou makest grow (*puṣyasi*) thy will (*kratum*)," and X, 75, 1, where "the craftsman in Vivasvan's seat shall, O ye Waters, tell of your incomparable all-might (*mahimānam uttamam*)." Hence also the designation of the "Rivers" as *revatī*, "rivers of plenty," X, 19, 1, etc.

In all probability the conch and lotus were originally symbols of the twain Waters: this would explain their association, as sources of inexhaustible wealth, with the *aśvattha*, in the case of the well-known Besnagar capital (my *Yakṣas*, II, pl. I, right): and their survival as the principal "treasures" (*nidhi*) of Kubera, Dhanapati, in whom the progenitive and plutocratic elements of Varuṇa's character are so clearly preserved.

[68] Thus in progenitive deities, especially Varuṇa, Brahmā, Kubera, and Gaṇapati, also in the case of the Patriarch and Prophet Agastya (twin of Vasiṣṭha, and like him probably = Prajāpati), the great belly is a symbol of pregnancy: such types embodying simultaneously chthonic (f.) and celestial (m.) powers. When Prakṛti is represented not thus as She is in him *nityayutau*, but as She is in herself, *ayuta*, in a wholly feminine form, then the promise of her infinite maternities is revealed more explicitly in her heavy breasts and swelling hips, told of in her litanies and seen in her images from prehistoric times to the present day. Clear indications of pregnancy are recognizable similarly in the iconography of mediæval Mariolatry.

[68a] On the connection between Intellect (*manas*) and the life of the body, see *Ṛg Veda*, X, 58, an incantation employed to recall the Intellect of a man at the point of death "that thou mayst live and sojourn here."

[69] Here the powers of the soul are called "angels," and all these leaving (*utkram*) the body at death, together with the five breaths (*prāṇa*), return to their source.

The root *kram* can be used in connection with any change of state ("all change is a dying"): do not only of procession, but also of recession, as in *Maitri Up.*, VI, 30, where *atikramya* is used with respect to ascession from Brahmaloka to the "final stage," *parama gati*.

[70] For example, when the Bodhisattva descends from the Tuṣita heaven to take birth on earth, Bārhat inscription *bhagavato ūkraṁti*, see Barua and Sinha, *Barhut inscriptions*, 1926, pp. 52-53. Cf. *Ṛg Veda*, I, 164, 19, "those had come hitherward (*arvañc*) they call departing (*parācaḥ*)."

[71] For the universal symbolism of the cross, see René Guénon, *La symbolisme de la Croix*, Paris, 1931. Observe also that the Cross is both a "tree" and a sacrificial "post." Similarly in Vedic texts the sacrificial post (*yūpa*) is often spoken of as a tree (*vanaspati*, "forest lord," *Ṛg Veda*, I, 13, 11; I, 65, 2; III, 8; X, 70, 10). As pointed out by Oldenberg, S.B.E., XLVI, p. 254, the ritual acts associated with the setting up of the sacrificial post "seem to be connected with ancient tree worship," cf. the accounts in *Śatapatha Brāhmaṇa*, III, 6, 4, and 7, 1. The three parts of the post, base, middle, and crest, correspond to the Three Worlds (ŚBr., III, 7, 1, 14 and 25), cf. *Bṛhadāraṇyaka Up.*, II, 2, 1, where the "new-born infant" (*śiśu* = the "Year" of our text) is compared to the sacrificial post, "his base (*ādhāna*, i.e., the part set into the earth) is this (Earth), his top (*pratyādhāna*) is (Heaven), his trunk (*sthūṇa*) midmost (*madhyamaḥ*) is Spirit (*prāṇa*), the fetter (*dāma*) food (*anna*)." The same simile is implied in *Aitareya Āraṇyaka*, II, 1, 6, where "language (*vāc*) is the rope (*tanti*), names its slip-knot (*dāma*) . . . whereby all things are bound." The rope and its knot by which the victim is held are more fully described in ŚBr., III, 7, 1, 19 and 20 as "triple" and as "food": it is bound about the navel of the post (*nābhidaghne*, *Taittirīya Saṁhitā*, VI, 3, 4, 5) and thought of as the clothing of the post. In ŚBr., loc. cit. and *Kauṣītaki Br.*, X, 1, the post is called a *vajra*. These passages taken together suffice to show that the sacrificial post was envisaged as the Tree of Life, the body of Prajāpati, its trunk the axis of the universe, the support of all existences, to "support existence" being indeed the very object of the sacrifice; and that which is the support of all existences is also the place of their extinction, at which the breaths of life are returned to their source, "*prāṇāḥ* to *prāṇa*" as the Vedas and Upaniṣads express what is

involved in our " dust to dust." To the arms of the Cross corresponds the rope of the sacrificial Post; both correspond to " felly " in the symbolism of the World-wheel. The details of these symbolisms are more fully discussed in my *Elements of Buddhist Symbolism*.

For representations of the Christian Cross as the Tree of Life, see Hildburgh, W. L., *A mediæval brass pectoral Cross*, Art Bulletin, XIV, 1932, pp. 79-102.

72 Whether or not the Comprehensor act-ually per-forms the ritual is a matter of indifference.

The concept of life itself (the "daily round ") as a ritual is expounded in *Chāndogya Up*., II, 17, concluding " Death is an ablution after the ceremony (*avabhṛta*)."

73 For *abhisambhava* see, e.g., *Chāndogya Up*., VIII, 13, " as a self perfected I am con-formed (*abhisambhavyāmi*) to the unmade world of Brahman." For *parāvṛtti*, e.g., of *maithuna*, cf. *Bṛhadāraṇyaka Up*., VI, 4, and Maitreya-Asanga, *Mahāyāna Sūtrâlaṅkāra*, IX, 46, also my *Parāvṛtti = transformation, regeneration, anagogy*, in Festschrift Ernst Winternitz, 1933.

Parāvṛtti, " transformation," " re-versal," should not be confused with *pariṇāma*, " permutation," which takes place in the order of nature.

To illustrate exactly what is meant by sublimation, transubstantiation or transformation " I see the lilies in the field, their gaiety, their colour, all their leaves . . . my outward man relishes creatures, as wine and bread and meat. But my inner man relishes things not as creature but as the gift of God. And again to my innermost man they savour not of God's gift but of ever and aye," Eckhart, I, 143. The change from one to another of these modes of perception constitutes a death of the soul.

74 No importance need be attached here to the " etymology " by which the word *aśva*, " horse," is connected with the root *śva*, " to swell." More plausible derivations are from *aś*, " to pervade," " wander wide," " range " ; or less probably, *aś*, " to eat," hence pre-eminently " to live."

75 " And so with works in God ; he thinks them and they are . . . he stays with creatures to keep them in being," Eckhart, I, 238 and 427. Cf. *Agni lokasmṛta*, " who remembers the worlds," *Maitri Up*., VI, 35. See also Note 59.

76 That would be in Sanskrit literally *prâṇasya nirvāṇa*, " despiration of the breath of life " : a re-turn (*nivṛtti*) to His modeless mode who " breathes without breathing," *ānīt avāta*, *Ṛg Veda*, X, 129, 2. Cf. *aprâṇa*, " spirit-less," or " despirited," *Muṇḍaka Up*., II, 1, 2.

77 *Yukta*, the *yogī*, " one who is uniformly-poised in heat and cold, pleasure and pain, repute and disrepute, etc.," *Bhagavad Gītā*, VI, 7 and 8, the same as Eckhart's " reasonable man "—" One who is controlled in joy and sorrow, him I call a reasonable man," I, 460, " unmoved by weal or woe or wealth or want," I, 56.

For the use of *yuj* in this sense, cf. *Ṛg Veda*, V, 46, 1, " Like a knowing horse I yoke myself (*svayam ayuji*) to the chariot pole, coveting neither liberation nor a coming back again " : a striking " anticipation " of " later " modes of thought.

78 *Ya evaṁ vedâhaṁ brahmâsmîti sa idaṁ sarvaṁ bhavati . . . yo'nyaṁ devatāmupāste'nyo sāvanyo'hamasmîti na sa veda, yathā paśurevaṁ sa devānām.*

79 Vedic ideas are types not of "things," but of acts; thus not exactly the same as Platonic ideas, but corresponding to the types of Aristotle as understood by the schoolmen. "Names are all derived from action," *Bṛhad Devatā*, I, 31, and *Nirukta*, VII, 4. "Because he creates the activity of everything (*viśva*), he is called Viśvakarma," *Bṛhad Devatā*, II, 50. The identity of *nāma* and *karma* as transmigrating factor is remarked by Keith, *Rel. and Phil.* of the Veda, p. 507: cf. also the opposition of *nāma* and *guṇa* in the *Mīmāṅsā* system. For the view that a thing is what it does, see also Vasubandhu, *Abhidharmakośa*, II, 56 d, Poussin, p. 289, and cf. *dharmā* (pl.) as "principles" and *dharma-cakra-pravartana* as equivalent to "utterance of the Word," *Saddharma Puṇḍarīka*, *passim*.

Nāma-rūpa, constituting the unity of the individual, are often rendered "name and form," but *nāma* is here the true "form": the combination *nāma-rūpa* really corresponds to "soul and body," as when, distinguishing form from substance, we say "the soul is the form of the body." *Nāma* = Lat. *forma*, Greek *eidos*; *rūpa* = Lat. *figūra*. Cf. Mainonides, *Guide* . . . III, 8, "Form can only be destroyed accidentally, i.e., on account of its connection with substance, the true nature of which consists in the property of never being without a disposition to receive form." Keith, *Aitareya Āraṇyaka*, p. 239, Note 2, remarks, "Even the Buddhist *rūpam* is not a pregnant conception." Of course not: the pregnant conception is *nāma*, *rūpa* being merely the sensible aspect. It is true that *rūpa*, like English "form," may be used with reference either to intelligible or to sensible objects, but when "informing form" is meant, *rūpa* is generally distinguished by a suitable determinant, as in *sva-rūpa*, "intrinsic form," or *antarjñeya rūpa*, "mental image." *Nāma* is noumenon, *rūpa* phenomenon.

80 The Indian similes of the Word-wheel and World-wheel, a mechanical but living image equivalent to that of the Cosmic Horse and World-tree, and more specifically representing the revolution of the "year," require a more detailed treatment than can be given here. Briefly, "we understand him as a wheel having a single felly, with a triple tire," *Śvetāśvatara Up.*, I, 4: a wheel, that is, of which the hub is essence and the felly nature, "triple" with respect to the three *guṇas*. Cf. Eckhart, I, 357, "This circle . . . is all the Trinity has ever wrought. Why is the work of the Trinity called a circle? Because the Trinity . . . is the origin of all things and all things return into their origin. This is the circle the soul runs. . . . So she goes round in endless chain. . . . Spent with her quest she casts herself into the centre. This point is the power of the Trinity wherein unmoved it is doing all its work. Therein the soul becomes omnipotent. . . . This is the motionless point and the unity of the Trinity. The circumference is the incomprehensible work of the Three Persons. . . . The union of the Persons is the essence of the point. In this point God runs through change without otherness, involving into unity of essence, and the soul as one with this fixed point is capable of all things." Or again, Eckhart, I, 56, "The heaven adjoining the eternal now, wherein the angels are, is motionless, immovable. . . . The heaven the sun is in, moved by angelic force, goes round once a year. The heaven the moon is in, again, is driven by angelic force and goes round once a month. The nearer the eternal now, the more immovable they are, the further off and more unlike to the eternal now the easier to move so that they are spinning in this temporal now . . . all things get their life and being from the motion there imparted by the eternal now."

[81] Cf. *Bṛhadāraṇyaka Up.*, V, 15, where the entrance (*mukha*) to the verity (*satya*) is said to be closed by the golden orb (*pātra*) and prayer is made to Pūṣan to discover that entrance to him whose principle (*dharma*) is the Verity (*satya*): and *Chāndogya Up.*, V, 10, 2, where a Superhuman Person (*amānava puruṣa*), who is Agni-vaidyuta, "of the Lightning," "leads them on to Brahman, this is the angelic voyage."

Similarly in the *Jaiminīya Upaniṣad Brāhmaṇa*, I, 5, passage is represented first as barred to the soul on ethical grounds, but when she answers to the Angel (Agni, or Agni-Rudra), "Thou it was, not 'I' that did the deeds," she proves herself a Comprehensor of the Self, proves that she is emancipate from individuality, proves that like her guide she is *amānava*, no longer thinking in human modes, and the way lies open. The doctrine as to "Works" of the *Bhagavad Gītā* is identical, though presented with some devotional colouring: thus, III, 30, "Casting off all thy works upon Me," IV, 13, "I (God) am the doer of works, but they defile Me not, who have no ends to be attained," IV, 36, "Even though thou be the most evildoer of all sinners, thou mayst by the ship of Understanding be brought across all evil," V, 10, "He who in doing works lays his works on Brahman and puts away attachment is undefiled," VI, 29, "Who sees Me in all things, and all things in Me, I am not lost to him nor he to me." These are metaphysical equivalents to the religious doctrines of forgiveness and remission of sins, salvation by faith, etc.: "Come unto Me, all ye that are weary and heavy laden (sc. with the burden of sin) and I will give you rest." If from the religious or ethical point of view it be objected that in the metaphysical formulation nothing is said about repentance, the answer is that that very Understanding by which the notion of individuality (*abhimāna*, etc.) is transformed, is in itself and quite literally a repentance, a turning-away-from (*nivṛtti*) these Worlds wherein alone are moral values valid.

[82] Union with Brahmā, or with the Buddha in Glory (Sambhogakāya), though it implies a sharing of the throne and sovereignty of God, is always clearly distinguished from emancipation (*mukti*, *nirvāṇa*), cf. Sāyaṇa on *Aitareya Āraṇyaka*, II, 3, 7 (citing also *Bṛhadāraṇyaka Up.*, IV, 1, 2) and Śaṅkarācārya on *Brahma Sūtra*, IV, 4, 22.

That is also made very clear in *Maitri Up.*, VI, 30, where the Comprehensor passes through the Solar region to the Brahma world and there beyond to the "ultimate station," *paraṁ gati*. In Buddhism, it is pointed out that even the highest of Buddha-paradises (Sambhogakāya-plane), is but a resting-place (*viśrāma*), not a Return (*nivṛti*) *Saddharma-Puṇḍarīka*, V, 74, 75. Similarly for Eckhart, I, 274, 276, the soul in heaven is "not yet dead and gone out into that which follows created existence . . . as this is not the summit of divine union, so it is not the soul's abiding place."

[83] "Lo, God de-spirited" (*aprāṇa*, *nir-vāta*), Eckhart, I, 469. Tirumūlar, "they lose themselves and become idle."

[84] Cf. *Bṛhadāraṇyaka Up.*, II, 4, 1, "it is for love of the Self alone that all things are dear": that is, "In the love wherein God loves himself therein he loves all things . . . in the joy wherein God enjoys himself, therein he enjoys all creatures," God is in all things self-intent, "the good man . . . formed in the image of God . . . loves for his own sake," Eckhart, I, 142, 380 and 66, "the love is to the lover and comes back most to him . . . itself only finally satisfies the soul," Walt Whitman.

[85] From Claude Field's version of selected *Sermons*, p. 28.

86 *Adornment of the Spiritual Marriage*, passim.

87 "That one breathes without stir," *ānīt avāta*, *Ṛg Veda*, X, 129, 2: "he sees without eyes," *paśyatyacakṣuḥ*, *Śvetāśvatara Up.*, III, 19; "sees without seeing," *paśyaty apaśyanayā*, *Saddharma Puṇḍarīka*, prose, p. 317. Other parallels could be cited.

88 Cf. *Ṛg Veda*, I, 115, 1, "the Sun (*sūrya*) is the Self (*ātman*) of all that proceeds or exists." Cf. Note 111.

88a "To consume food" is a general expression for "to exist." "This indeed is the premier aspect (*paraṁ rūpam*) of the Self, viz., 'food' (*anna*), for Spirit (*prāṇa*) indeed is mode-ified (*-maya*) by 'food' . . . from 'food' are all-things-begotten that-abide-on-any-ground verily begotten, by 'food' in sooth they live, and thereto in their latter end return," *Maitri Up.*, VI, 11. Nature, from whom all things "milk" their specific virtue, is the ultimate, Earth the proximate source of "food,"—"through Me alone (viz., *Vāc*) all eat the food that feeds them—each man who sees, breathes, hears the Word outspoken," *Ṛg Veda*, X, 125. Needless to say that the symbol "food" has the widest possible reference, implying not merely comestibles, but whatsoever nourishes the ego in any way, spiritually, mentally, or physically: cf., "eating of the Tree" in Genesis, and in *Ṛg Veda*, I, 164, 20. *Annāt bhavanti bhūtāni . . . parjanyāt . . . yajnāt karmaṇaḥ*, *Bhagavad Gīta*, III, 14.

89 Eckhart, I, 81, "the intellect wherein there is measureless space, wherein I am as near a place a thousand miles away as the place I am standing on this moment . . . (where) a hundred is as one."

90 *Ṛg Veda*, III, 62, 10.

91 Cf. *Ṛg Veda*, IX, 113, 6 and 7, *yatra brahmā . . . yatra jyotir ajasraṁ*, "where Brahmā is, there Light is emanated." Also *Bṛhad Devatā*, VII, 109, "that knowledge (*jñāna*) which is immortal Light, and by union wherewith one wins to Brahman."

92 Cf. *Ṛg Veda*, IV, 13, 5, "Unsupported, unattached, spread-out downwards-turned": and *ibid.*, I, 24, 7, "King Varuṇa upholds in the abyss (*abudhna*, firmament, cf. VIII, 77, 5) as Pure-Act (Dakṣa) the summit (*stūpa*) of the Tree (*vana*), the ground (*budhna*) is above, may its downward-standing flaming-banners (*ketavaḥ*) be planted-deep (*nihitaḥ*) in us."

92a The notion of an Imperishable-Word (*akṣara*) by which the earth is measured out appears in *Ṛg Veda* X, 13, 3.

92b The notions of the Tree of Life, Pillar of Smoke, and Axis of the Universe are all closely connected. Cf., for example, *Ṛg Veda*, IV, 6, 2, *metaiva dhumaṁ stabhāyat upa dhyām*, "He (Agni) as a pillar of smoke upholds the heavens" (Sāyaṇa explains *metā* as *sthūṇā*). Agni, again, is often spoken of as Vanaspati, flames being his branches.

93 "How in the beginning this world was not, either as non-existent or existent, how all this was born (*jajñe*), that (i.e., a hymn of that kind) they term the 'movement of being' (*bhāva vṛtta*) (hymn)." *Vṛtta*, also implying "circle," "cycle," "transformation," "appearance," eventuality," "activity," etc., is from root *vṛt*, "to move," "revolve," "proceed," "exist," etc. (or with similar senses causatively), which root is also present in *vartana*, *cakravartin*, with reference to the setting in motion of the world-wheel, and in *pravṛtti*, *nivṛtti*, "extroversion" and "introversion," or "evolution" and "involution." Certain of the hymns of the *Ṛg Veda*, e.g., X, 129, are *bhāva vṛttāni*, cf. *Bṛhad*

Devatā, II, 86, VII, 123, VIII, 46 and 91; in VIII, 56, *Ṛg Veda*, X, 145, is called an *aupaniṣuda bhāva vṛtta* hymn, which is rendered by Macdonell as "esoteric evolutional hymn."

[94] *Upaniṣad* as a verb with the sense "to sit near" (with a view to hearing a discourse, as we speak of sitting under a lecturer) may be noted in *Jaiminīya Upaniṣad Brāhmaṇa*, III, 3, 7, and *Aitareya Brāhmaṇa*, II, 2, 3.

Bloomfield, in J.A.O.S., XV, 144, argues "that *mantra* and *brāhmaṇa* are for the least part chronological distinctions; that they represent two modes of literary activity, and two modes of literary speech, which are largely contemporaneous. . . . Both forms existed together, for aught we know, from earliest times." Needless to remark that *brāhmaṇa* includes, to a certain degree, *upaniṣad*.

It may be stated as a law, that a given traditional text represents no more than a comparatively late fixation and publication of doctrines long previously taught orally. *Cf*. *Śatapatha Brāhmaṇa*, XIV, 1, 1, 26 and 27, and *Muṇḍaka Up.*, I, 2, 12 and 13; and the lists of teachers in pupillary succession, e.g., *Bṛhadāraṇyaka Up.*, II, 6.

With the distinction between the Vedic *saṁhitās* on the one hand and the Brāhmaṇas and Upaniṣads on the other, may be compared the distinction between the Babylonian liturgies "repeated in the temples" and the "wisdom literature . . . not written to be repeated in the temples"; this wisdom literature "shows an increasing scepticism concerning the value of this life," and whereas "life unto distant days," in Babylonian liturgies, like *amṛta* in *Ṛg Veda*, X, 129, 2, may have meant rather fullness of life and length of days than "immortality," it was precisely in the wisdom literature and especially towards the end of the Babylonian empire that there was developed a "doctrine of final escape from mortality," Langdon, S., *Tammuz and Ishtar*, pp. 11, 14, 38, 41.

[95] The "appearance of polytheism" is a secondary development in tradition, and this development *had already taken place antecedently to the Vedas as we possess them*. What Professor Langdon has to say of the Sumero-Accadian pantheon is absolutely pertinent, viz., "The complicated Sumerian pantheon was obviously the work of theologians and of gradual growth. Almost all the names of deities express . . . some personification of natural powers, ethical or cultural functions, perfectly intelligible to the Sumerologist . . . names given to definite mythological conceptions by clear thinking theologians and accepted in popular religion. . . . Since in their mythology all the gods descended from An, the Sky-god, it is extremely probable that the priests who constructed the pantheon were monotheists at an earlier stage, having only the god An, a word which actually means 'high' . . . (that is) not a mythology springing from primitive religion, but speculation based upon nature, spiritual, and ethical values," *Semitic mythology*, p. 89. Cf. "le monde des dieux (sc. the Āditya-maṇḍala) relativement homogène a l'origine, se soit differencié plus tard," Przyluski, *Brahmā Sahāmpati*, Journal Asiatique, CCV, 1924, pp. 155-163.

The "abstract deities" of Vedic scholarship, for example, represent essential names not yet divided from their source and independently personalised: a multiplication of deities, or rather of angels, takes place by a gradual treatment of essential names as though these had been personal designations, as for example in the case of Kāma, Viśvakarma, Tvaṣṭṛ, Prajāpati.

96 All symbols are "according to the enlightenment of the reason of him who shapes and shows them," Ruysbroeck.

97 *Kavi*, from root *kū*, to voice, utter (= *kav*, to describe or depict), is in Vedic usage nearly synonymous with words such as *ṛṣi*, *sumedha*, *dhīra*, *rebha*, "prophet," "sage," "singer." The professional reference to "one who makes literature," and the application of the term *kāvya* to "belle-lettres" belong to a later time. If we render the word *kavi* by "poet," we must do so with the original meaning of *poiein*, to "make," "create," in view, and think of the poet not as lyricist, but as shaper, maker, prophet, oracle, or Latin *vates*, or even as a magician in the proper sense. Vedic poetry is neither "fine" nor "decorative," but simply highly accomplished in execution; the "poet" rightly compares his own craftsmanship to that of the weaver or wheelwright, in modern terms we might say to engineering rather than to "art." The verses (*ṛc*) or measures (*chandas*) are thought of as formulæ, spells, incantations, centres of force or words of power (*mantra*). They are not in any way comparable to hymns or prayers such as are now thought of as the natural expression of "religious" aspiration: for the operation of a Vedic rite or hymn depends on accurate performance, not on any emotional state on the part of the celebrant, or emotional response on the part of the object of "worship." What is truly moving in Vedic "poetry" is not a lyrical quality, but one of profundity: the lauds are means to happiness far rather than to pleasure, and it would be an affectation to speak of them as "literature." "What is set forth in the Vedas, that is Essential Truth. By what the Vedas tell, wise men live their life," *Maitri Up.*, VII, 10.

The Vedas are not of human origin, but *apauruṣeya*, Śaṅkarâcārya on the *Vedânta Sūtra*, I, 2, 2. On the one hand the utterance of the mantras and ordering of the ritual ("the observance of the rule thereof is the same as at the 'creation,'" *Śatapatha Brāhmaṇa*, XIV, 1, 2, 26 and XIV, 3, 1, 36) by the Angels or by non-individual Prophets, Poets, or Seers, represents a co-creative activity whereby the one and singular Utterance of the Spirit is contracted and identified (*vi dhā*, *Ṛg Veda*, X, 71, 3) into variety (*viśvam*): the discrimination of things by name (*nāma-dheya Ṛg Veda*, X, 71, 1, see Note 62) being the immediate cause of their distinction as such, cf. the statement of Śaṅkarâcārya, *Vedânta Sūtra*, I, 1, 3, that the Veda "is the cause of the distinction (*paribhāga-hetu*) of the castes and estates of angels, animals, and men." So we have in *Ṛg Veda*, X, 5, 2, "Poets (*kavi*) ward the traces (*pada*) of the Law-of-Heaven (*ṛta*), and in the innermost (*guhā*) are-pregnant-with (*dhṛ*) the ultimate (*para*) ideas (*nāma*)": X, 71, 1, "Then what was best and flawless in them, hid in the innermost, that by their love they brought to light." The *Nirukta*, XII, 13, with reference to the designation of Savitṛ, the Solar Angel, as *kavi*, in *Ṛg Veda*, V, 81, 2, explains, "He is *kavi* in that he displays (or reveals, lit., releases) the various forms-of-things (*viśvā rūpāṇi prati muñcate*) . . . '*kavi*,' either because his presence is desired (√ *kam*), or the word is derived from √ *kav*, to describe, praise, or depict." How, then, the designation *kavi* is appropriate to the Sun and to the prophet alike is, inasmuch as both reveal or bring to light, that is into the field of perception, what was previously unseen or latent.

On the other hand, by the reverse process implied in the phrase "for him who understands," the *mantras* constitute a means of reunion to higher states of consciousness. We might express this in Vedic phraseology by saying that the yarn of the poetic tissue can be traced intellectually back to its unitary source, or that the metres are traces of footprints of the Law and may be followed on a homeward course, just as a lost animal is tracked. It is from this standpoint of a return from existence to its sources in pure Being and Non-being that the Vedic texts are considered in the Upaniṣads.

[98] Cf. *Viṣṇu Purāṇa*, I, 8, 23, *padmā svadhā śāśvatapuṣṭidā*, "the Lotus-Lady (= Śrī-Lakṣmī = Prakṛti = Māyā) is intrinsic-power, constant giver of increase"; also the discussion of Aditi, Māyā, Virāj, above, p. 31f. *Ṛg Veda*, X, 129, 5, corresponds exactly to Dante, *Paradiso*, XXIX, 31-36, "Co-created and in-wrought with the Substances was Order; which were the summit of the world, wherein pure Act was put forth. Pure Potentiality held the lowest place; in the midst Potentiality twisted such a withy with Act as shall ne'er be unwithied," where also *nel cima del mondo*, *mezzo*, and *infime parte* correspond to Vedic "celestial," "atmospheric," and "terrestrial." *Sustanzie*, "substances," here refers to the Angels, cf. *Paradiso*, XXIX, 76-78, who primarily fulfil the act of being: *concreato* and *construtto* correspond to the *ekajātatva*, *sālokyatva*, etc., of the *Bṛhad Devatā*, cited above, pp. 64, 65, and Note 113.

[99] "Neither can exist without the other, so neither can originate the other," Eckhart, I, 479.

Cf. Jīlī, "I am convinced that It is non-existence, since by existence It was manifested, thought hath beheld it from afar as a power exerting itself in existence. . . . It is the hidden treasure," Nicholson, *Studies* . . . p. 89.

[100] Cf. Keith, *Religion and philosophy of the Veda*, pp. 539, 540. For the view that the *guṇa* theory is substantially of much greater antiquity, and extra-Vedic origin, see Przyluski, J., *La théorie des guṇa*, Bull. Sch. Or. Studies, VI, pp. 24-35.

Rajas in *Pañcaviṁśa Brāhmaṇa*, XVIII, 7, 11, is again simply "*antarikṣa*": Sāyaṇa very rightly speaks of the meaning here as "obvious," and Caland's discussion in his *Pañcaviṁśa Brāhmaṇa*, 1931, p. 488, is quite superfluous. In *Ṛg Veda*, V, 47, 3, unquestionably, *rajas* = *antarikṣa*: for Heaven and Earth are its limits (*antāḥ*).

[101] For *tejas* = *sattva*, see Sénart, E., *La théorie des guṇas*, Études Asiatiques, II, pp. 287-292. Further, as has been shown by Hertel in particular, *tejas* = *vareṇya* (= *hvarcna*) = *brahma*.

[102] See above, pp. 32, 57, and my *On translation: maya, deva, tapas*, in Isis, No. 55. "The Godhead is contained in the Father as essence, *wherefore he is omnipotent* . . . the potentiality of the essence lies in *not* being a rational Person: in persisting in its essential unity," Eckhart, I, 373 and 393, italics mine. The pertinence of these considerations to modern therapeutic psychology and the resolution of "conflicts" will not be overlooked. Virtuosity and spontaneity in action (*agibile* and *factibile*, Skr. *karma*), better than obedience to rules externally imposed, better than to obey the "dictates" of the "conscience," are commonly exemplified in the shining of the sun, who shines *only* because that is its *nature*, and not for any "sake." Such a virtuosity and spontaneity can only be realised to the extent that we abandon purpose and let the divine nature work in us: "Let go thyself and let God work in thee," Eckhart, I, 308. That is the principle of *wu wei*, Chuang Tzŭ's "Do nothing, and all things shall be done"; that is the doctrine of the *Bhagavad Gītā* with respect to works. In *bhaktivāda* terms that is called the resignation of the will, *asaktatva*, *islām*: resulting in a "grace" or power which robs the ego of self-willing and self-thinking and substitutes therefor His will who is without potentiality (in the sense

that all potentiality is realised in him, cf. Eckhart, I, 409). With respect to *agibilia* and *factibilia*, we call this grace *habitus*, Skr., *kauśalya*, *ślistatva* (cf. my *Reactions to Art in India*, J.A.O.S., Vol. 52, p. 220, note 10, third paragraph). "It behoves a man in all he does to turn his will in God's direction and keeping only God in view to forge ahead without a qualm, not wondering, am I right or am I doing something wrong? If the painter had to plan out every brush-mark before he made his first he would not paint at all. And if, going to some place, we had first to settle how to put the front foot down, we should never get there," Eckhart, I, 141. Cf. St. Thomas, "human virtues are habits," *Sum. Th.*, II, Q. 55, A. 2. To identify this point of view with "nature-worship" (where "nature" stands for "ens naturata"), to suppose that what is meant by all this is nothing but a "selfish" obedience to merely functional impulses and animal instincts, implies a defective intellect: for how can he, who is by definition freed from private will, be at the same time spoken of as "self-willed"? As remarked by Jung, *Psychological types*, p. 263, "as we study the Upanishad philosophy, the impression grows on us that the attainment of the path is not just the simplest of tasks." Proportionate to the difficulty of the task, however, is the immediate reward in terms of power and happiness, which power and happiness are precisely from the Upaniṣad point of view, the values of gnosis.

103 With *dadhe* in this active sense of "appointed," cf. *dharmāni dadhiṣe Ṛg Veda*, IX, 64, 1; also X, 81, 5, *vidhātṛ*.

104 "To compare" (the "first existing one thing, which is described as breathing without wind") with "Aristotle's deity, the unmoved mover, is to falsify entirely primitive thought": similarly, the "assertion that the sages were able to discriminate between the thing in itself and the phenomenal world, between *natura naturans* and *natura naturata*" is unnatural and strained," Keith, *Religion and philosophy of the Veda*, p. 436. Professor Keith himself does not understand the type of thought he is discussing. *Pamāṇaṁ na jānāsi*, *Jātaka*, II, 254; *cikituṣe janāya, mā gām anāgām aditiṁ vadhiṣṭa*, *Ṛg. Veda*, VIII, 101, 15.

When the modern scholar boldly asserts that "the method of interpreting earlier ideas from a larger point of view," that is to say in the light of our own deeper understanding, may be "very serviceable . . . to the expounder of a philosophy or to the exhorter of a religion . . . yet by the scholar is to be carefully discriminated from a historically correct exegesis of the primitive statements" (Hume, *Thirteen Upanishads*, p. 299, Note 2), there comes to mind a remark of the *pṛthagjana* very often overheard in museums in presence of the Italian "primitives," "That was before they knew anything about anatomy." The notion of "progress" in fact so flatters our pride, that we cannot refrain from applying it even where it is inapplicable, i.e., in the fields of art and metaphysics. Professor Hume's own versions and induction of the Upaniṣads raise in our minds very serious doubts of his own "larger point of view."

105 When Professor Keith speaks of "our natural desire to modernise and to find reason prevailing in a barbarous age," he begs the whole question, and we suggest, again to quote his own words, that "we must be prepared to shed our personal predilections and to accept the conclusion which evidence indicates" (*Buddhist philosophy*, p. 26). Those who think that "in a country like this we must not expect to find anything that appeals to mind or to deep feeling" (Baden-Powell,

Panjab manufactures, 1872, II, iii) are not likely to be disappointed by the results of their researches, the only marvel is why they undertake them at all. In the case of those who devote their lives to a study of the Vedas, despite an *a priori* conviction of their spiritually negligible content, one may well ask *yastanna veda kimṛcā kariṣyati?* (*Ṛg Veda*, I, 164, 39 = *Śvetāśvatara Up.*, IV, 8). What in fact can the Veda mean for these? *Ta ete vācam abhipadya pāpayā sirīstantraṁ tanvate aprajajñayaḥ*, *Ṛg Veda*, X, 71, 9.

It is hardly possible for the western scholar to realise that the very terms applied by themselves to Vedic texts (e.g., "puerile, arid, and inane," said of the Brāhmaṇas, Lanmann, *Sanskrit Reader*, p. 357), are precisely those in which their own exegetical productions are evaluated by the most competent Indian scholars, who are either too polite to say what they think, or politic enough to play the game of western scholarship by way of condescension to the *pratyakṣa-priyatā* of the present day and age.

The western scholar (e.g., Lanmann, *ibid.*, 356, 357) complains that "what we deem the realities of life" are for the Brahmanical thinker "mere shadows" (and so at least puts the Brahman in a class with Plato and others of his rank): and that for the Brahman "Everything is not only that which it *is* but also what it *signifies*" (and so ranks the Brahman with Deity or Buddha, for whose omniscience "all principles are *same*"). The Indian thinker may be insufficiently arrogant to accept such praise, but he is at least sufficiently intellectual to understand that one in whom "the line of demarcation between 'is' and 'signifies' becomes almost wholly obliterated" cannot be far from His "omnipotence and salvation" in whom the distinction of Essence from Nature is *altogether* obliterated.

It is not without reason that Jung confesses "Our western air of superiority in the presence of Indian understanding is a part of our essential barbarism" (*Psychological types*, p. 263), or that as Salmony remarks, "Man darf ruhig sagen: Das europäische Urteil wurde bisher durch den Drang nach Selbstbehauptung verfälscht" (*Die Rassenfrage in der Indienforschung*, Sozialistische Monatsheften, 8, 1926).

[106] *Uttānapad*, "with feet outstretched": cf. *nyunnutānaḥ* "downwards extended," *Ṛg Veda*, IV, 13, 5. Or if *uttāna* = *uttānā* = *pṛthvī*, "Earth-outspread," then *uttānapad* would be equivalent to *supratiṣṭha* "firmly supported" in the possibilities of existence, of. *supratiṣṭhapāda*, Maitreya-Asanga, *Uttaratantra*, II, 16. In *Ṛg Veda*, I, 164, 33, both Heaven and Earth are "*uttāna*."

[107] Dakṣa, Tvaṣṭṛ, Viśvakarma, properly essential names of God with respect to his creative activity, are called by Vedic scholars as "Abstract gods," and seem to be regarded by them as independent personalities. To create an adequate parallel, for example in Christian theology, we should have to regard Jehovah, the Father, the Creator, the Lord of Hosts, etc., and likewise Jesus and Christ as distinct "gods," with solemn discussion of their diverse ethnic origins and oppositions. Vedic and later authors on the other hand are perfectly aware of the identities; for example, that Tvaṣṭṛ is the same as Savitṛ, Viśvakarma, and Prajāpati: as is indeed perfectly evident from the Vedic accounts of Tvaṣṭṛ's personality and functions. To conceive of Aditi, Nirṛti, Urvaśī, Lakṣmī, etc., as distinct "goddesses" would be equally misleading. Umā, Pārvatī, Durgā, Kālī, etc., are by no means distinct essences, one more or less abstract than another.

Dakṣa = *dúnamis*, Dante's *puro atto nel cima del mondo*: *Aditi* = *energeia*, Dante's *potenza in infime parte*.

[108] Not that either *originates* the other, but that neither can *be* without the other.

[109] The theme is further developed in *Aitareya Āraṇyaka*, II, 1, 5, where *satya* is treated as threefold, just as the OM is a + u + m: here "*sat* is Spirit, *ti* is Food (the *means* of being in a mode), and *tya* is yonder Supernal-Sun: that (*satya*) is triple." The sentence following, which arouses Keith's moral indignation (*Aitareya Āraṇyaka*, 1909, p. 207, Note 8), is perfectly intelligible in the light of the concluding part of *Bṛhadāraṇyaka Up.*, V, 5, 1, to be translated as follows: (1) "Though he speaks amiss (*mṛṣā*), yet he speaks Truth (*satya*) who knows this Truthfulness of Truth (*satyasya satyattvam*)." and (2) "The first and last syllables are Truth (*satya*), in the midst is the Untrue (*anṛta*). This Untrue is comprehended on both sides by the Truth, so the Truth preponderates. The Untruth does not injure him who knoweth this." Neither passage envisages an ethical problem of any sort: both are dealing with the metaphysically True and Untrue, *Vidyā* and *Avidyā*. He who understands that "Brahman is all this," that Multiplicity is merely the becoming, the middle term of the Unity, though he may (as indeed he must) use the language of empiricism, is not deceived, misled, or injured thereby, for he knows contingent things eternalwise, he is not really but only apparently a "materialist," all his "facts" are transformed by his understanding of them.

As for the moral crux apparently presented by passages such as *Kauṣitaki Up.*, III, 1, see above, p. 95. The *jīvanmukta*, by hypothesis, having no motives, cannot be charged with good or evil purposes, "such, indeed, do nothing for themselves," *Prem Sāgar*, Ch. XXXIV. Or according to Deussen's "acute and concise interpretation" (Hume), ignored by Keith, "Whoever has attained the knowledge of the Ātman and his unity with it, and thereby has been delivered from the illusion of individual existence, his good and evil deeds come to nought: they are no longer his deeds, simply because he is no longer an individual" (*Sechzig Upanisads des Veda*, p. 144, Note 1).

It was also the view of Aristotle that he who surpasses his fellows beyond all comparison in virtue is a law to himself, and not to be judged by other laws. Perfection and morality are incommensurable terms. If any are alarmed by this proposition, let them reflect that this doctrine by no means excepts the Wayfarer from his obligations, "while we are on the way we are not there," and that any man who claims to be a Comprehensor, or in a state of Grace, does so at his own peril. That there can be false prophets does not affect the doctrine as to the intrinsic form of Perfection: which form, by its very nature, must be inexpressible in terms of thesis and antithesis, good or evil.

Eckhart, "No law is given to the righteous, because he fulfils the law inwardly, and bears it in himself" (Claud Field's selected *Sermons*, p. 55); St. Augustine, "Love God, and do what you will."

On Perfection and Liberty, see Guénon, *Les états multiples de l'être*, 1932, Ch. XVIII, and *L'homme et son devenir selon le vedanta*, Chs. XXIV and XXVI. That should be compared with the whole of *Bṛhadāraṇyaka Up.*, II, 3, where for example, the quintessence or tincture (*rasa*) of the "yon" is said to be the Person in the Sun. Cf. also Note 37a.

[110] "Anything known or born is an image," Eckhart, I, 258. Rāmānuja glosses *mūrta* by *kaṭhina*, "concrete."

[111] The usual implication of *sthā* is "to exist," i.e., as natural species, any "thing": nor is this at all inconsistent with Rāmānuja's

gloss, *sthita* = *avyāpaka*, "particular," "individual," in opposition to *yat* = *vyāpaka*, "universal," "pervading." The common renderings (Max Müller, Hume, etc.) of *sthita* as "solid" or "stationary," are entirely misleading, the reference being to whatever is integrated or actual, whether physical or mental. In the same way the renderings of *yat* as "fluid" or "moving" are mistaken: "fluids" are by no means less "*sthita*" than are "solids," while the "mobility" implied in *yat* is principial, not local. As remarked by Sāyaṇa in connection with *Ṛg Veda*, V, 19, 1, *sthitaṁ padārtha jātam*, "the meaning of the word *sthita* is 'born'," cf. Eckhart, "Anything known or born is an image," as in *Bṛhadāraṇyaka Up.*, II, 3, 1, where what is *sthita* is also *mūrta*. What is *sthita*, existent, is precisely the five subtle elements and their gross manifestations: "this all, this work of His which revolves, is to be thought of as solid (*pṛthvya*), liquid (*āpya*), phlogistical (*teja*), gaseous (*anila*) and etheric (*kha*)," *Śvetāśvatara Up.*, VI, 2.

Sthita is to *yat* as *tasthuṣaḥ* to *jagataḥ* in *Ṛg Veda*, I, 115, 1; as *dhruva* to *carat* in X, 5, 3 (*dhruva* = *sthita* also in VII, 88, 7); as *tiṣṭhatu* to *anugāta* in X, 19, 3 and 1 (where also *sthā* in 3 corresponds to *jiv* in 6); as *ejat* to *carat* in *Muṇḍaka Up.*, II, 1 (where the "*carat*" is *guhā sannihitam*, "hid in the innermost"); and as *paribhramati* to *carati* in *Maitri Up.*, III, 2 and II, 7 (where also that which "*carati*" is *acala*, "immoveable"). In *Maitri Up.*, VI, 6, *car* is used with respect to the Person in the eye, which "surveys" (*carati*) dimensioned things. In all these passages *gam* and *car* are used with respect to principial motion, *sthā* with respect to things which have a place and local motion; cf. Eckhart, I, 114, "Like motion without motion although causing motion and size which has no size though the principle of size."

The case of *Ṛg Veda*, V, 47, 5, is especially interesting: "'Tis a marvel, this paradox, ye folk, that when the rivers (*nadyaḥ*) flow (*caranti*), the waters (*āpaḥ*) stand (*tasthuḥ*)." Direct comparison with Ecclesiastes, I, 7, is fallacious. What is intended is as follows: Principial motion *there*, is birth, concrete existence, position, *here*."

112 See my *On translation*: *maya*, *deva*, *tapas*, in Isis, 55. A minimum qualification for a profound study of this aspect of Vedic ontology would be not merely a knowledge of the Vedas and Upaniṣads, but in addition an acquaintance with the Gnostic conception of the Pleroma and of Aeons, and with the Christian theory of angels as outlined in the sections of the *Summa Theologica* dealing with Divine Government (I, QQ. 103-119). The discussion above is offered merely as an essay towards a better understanding of the problems involved.

113 Cf. also *Bṛhad Devatā*, I, 98, "the divinity (*devatva*) of each angel is from their *being-of-one-sphere* (*sālokyatva*) and of one and the same origin (*ekajātatva*) and because of the immanence (*vyāptimatva*) of the fiery-energy (*tejas*) in them, though it is seen that they are individually lauded." A like interdependence of the angels is implied in the *susamrabdha* of our text. The "angels" here are the Persons of the Trinity.

114 Inversely, the angel is the "self" (*ātman*) of the weapon or vehicle, *Bṛhad Devatā*, IV, 143.

115 That is, each of the Selves or Persons has his own-nature, potentiality, *śakti*.

116 The discussion above covers only one of the numerous classes of angels; actually the hosts (*gaṇa*) of the angels include beside the Viśve Devāḥ, also the Ādityas, Vasus, Mahārājikas, Sādhyas and others. In *Taittirīya Up.*, II, 8, three hierarchies of angels are referred to, of whom the highest are simply "Angels" (*devāḥ*), and next to these are the "angels with respect to works" (*karma-devāḥ*), "who reach the angels by their works" (*ye karmaṇā devānapyanti*) evidently the same as the "angels whose self is works" (*karmātmanāḥ devāḥ*) of the *Mānava Dharmaśāstra*, I, 22; third in rank are the "begotten angels" (*ājānajāḥ devāḥ*), and all these are superior to the Patriarchs (*pitaraḥ*). In the words of Dionysius, "our knowledge of the angels is imperfect" (*Coel. Hier.*, VI).

It can hardly be doubted that Williams Jackson, J.A.O.S., Vol. 21, pp. 168 and 181, rightly interprets Avestan *vītha* as derived from *vīspa* (Skr. *viśva*) "all," and that the "All-gods" often mentioned in connection with Ahura Mazda were precisely the "Several Angels" of Vedic texts.

117 With further reference to "Dakṣa": the two posthumous voyages, *devayāna* and *pitṛyāna* are described in the Upaniṣads as respectively "northern" (*uttara*) and "southern" (*dakṣiṇa*). Observe now that *uttara* means primarily "yonder," "higher," "transcendent," etc., *dakṣiṇa* primarily "of or belonging to Dakṣa," the meanings northern and southern being secondary. Dakṣa's "way" is precisely that of the *pitṛyāna* (inasmuch as he is himself by his works and sacrifice the cause of his own return to embodied existence at the dawn of every "creation") and that is why the *pitṛyāna* is called *dakṣiṇa*, "southern."

118 Note that *yajña* = *dulia*, *pūjā* = *latria*. *Yajña*, "sacrifice," is properly speaking a metaphysical (or as anthropologists express it, "magical"), not a devotional rite. The bull sacrifice in Atlantis, described by Plato (*Krit*, 119 D and E) well illustrates what is meant by "a metaphysical rite." The Greek Bouphonia (for which, with its significance, see Harrison, *Themis*, 2nd ed., pp. 141 ff.) very closely parallels the Indian Aśvamedha; both are "mimetic representations," *apomimema*. And just as the Aśvamedha was later claimed by Indra, so the Bouphonia by Zeus, in reality both sacrifices antedate anthropomorphic conceptions of deity. If Christian *dulia* now implies devotion, that is only what took place elsewhere, in Greece and India alike, the figure of an anthropomorphic deity being as it were superimposed upon the original formula, in accordance with the requirements of the religious (devotional) extension of the original "mystery."

An excellent example of a metaphysical (certainly not a "religious") rite may be instanced in the Vājapeya ceremonies, where ritual racing takes place, and the sacrificer mounts the sacrificial post, cf. *Pañcaviṁśa Brāhmaṇa*, XVIII, 7, 9 and 10, "They run a race course, and make the Sacrificer win; thereby they make him gain the world of heaven. He mounts to the sky; to the world of heaven he thereby ascends." All Vedic rites are of this sort, viz., that described by anthropologists as "magical."

An admirable account of a metaphysical rite may be found in H. Blodget, *The worship of Heaven and Earth by the Emperor of China*, J.A.O.S., XX, 58 ff.

119 "What are opposites? Good and bad, white and black are in opposition, a thing which has no place in real being," Eckhart, I, 207.

120 Thus, "He uses the demons for Himself," St. Thomas, *Sum. Th.*, I, Q. 109, A. 1.

121 Cf. *Ṛg Veda*, II, 5, 2, *manuṣvāt daivyam aṣṭamām*, "the eighth angelic being in human guise"; I, 35, 6-9, where it is Savitṛ that lights the world and eight airts. The best list of eight Ādityas occurs in *Taittirīya Āraṇyaka*, I, 13, 3, where the eighth (Vivasvat) is identified with Martāṇḍa, i.e., Āditya as manifested and existent deity, the others seem to be Mitra, Varuṇa, Aryamān, Dakṣa, Bhāga, Aṁśa, and Agni or Soma, cf. S.B.E., XXXII, 252 f.

122 Aeon, "a power existing from eternity . . . phase of the supreme deity taking part in the creation and government of the universe," New English Dictionary. Pleroma, in the New Testament, is the "fullness" of Deity, cf. *pūrṇa* and *kṛtsna* in the Upaniṣads, and *akṛtsna*, "not entire," characterising individual existence, e.g., *Bṛhadāraṇyaka Up.*, I, 4, 7; in Valentianian gnosticism, likewise, the Pleroma is the abode of the Angels.

Cf. de la Vallée Poussin's exegesis of *Dharmakāya* and *Sambhogakāya* as primary and secondary "Aeons," J.R.A.S., 1906, p. 967.

123 Similarly Chinese *yu t'ien*.

The return of the seven Ādityas to the Empyrean recalls Irenaeus, III, 11, 1, "the Christ from above . . . continued impassible . . . (and after descending upon Jesus) flew back into his Pleroma."

124 Cf. *Ṛg Veda*, X, 13, 4, "He for weal (*kam*) of the Angels chose death (*mṛtyu*), and for the weal of their begotten chose not immortality (*amṛta*): they sacrificed the Prophet, Bṛhaspati, Yama yielded up his own dear body."

Cf. the creative transformation of Dionysos described as a "rending asunder" and "tearing limb from limb," Plutarch, *de Ei ap. Delph*, IX. Is a scene of this kind to be recognized in the Sumerian seal illustrated by Legrain, Museum Journal, Sept.-Dec., 1929, Pl. XL, No. 111?

125 A further argument might perhaps be developed from the fact that in the *Śulbasūtra*, *uttara yuga* represents a particular measurement, viz., *trayodaśaṅgulam*.

126 "There in that all-possessing-all-pervading (*prāpti-*) form of Virāj, in the primordial Empyrean (*nāke pūrve*) the Saints (*sādhyāḥ*), who were of old (*purātanāḥ*) worshippers (*sādhakāḥ*) of the Virāj, now-abide (*santi tiṣṭhanti*): they dwell-in (*sacanta*) that Empyrean, the all-possessing-all-pervading form of Virāj, in Paradise (*svargam*), as Powers-attendant-thereon (*mahimānastadupāsakāḥ*), as Mighty-Selves (*mahātmānaḥ*, 'Mahatmas')," cf. *Chāndogya Up.*, III, 10, and *Bhagavad Gītā*, X, 15.

127 No "gliding down," *avaprabhraṁśana* in the *Atharva Veda*, XIX, 39, 8, *avasarpaṇa* in the *Śatapatha Brāhmaṇa*, I, 8, I, 7, *punar avṛtti* and *punar apādana*, Upaniṣads, *passim*, *āvṛttam punaḥ*, *Ṛg Veda*, V, 46, 1.

128 In *Aitareya Brāhmaṇa*, II, 4, 3 (Ait. Up., I, 3, 13 and 14), Indra ("Idamdra") is plainly an epithet (essential name) of the Self (Ātman). Cf. *Ṛg Veda*, V, 3, 1, "Thou (Agni, Varuṇa, Mitra) art Indra to the mortal worshipper."

129 Cf. my *Yakṣas*, II, pp. 26, 27.

130 As is often the case in the *Ṛg Veda*, e.g., III, 23, 2 and 3. Cf. Indra identified with Prajāpati and the Person in the Sun,

Kauṣītaki Br., VIII, 3; and Indra as Glory (*yaśas*) and Lord of Existences (*bhūtānām-adhipati*), *Aitareya Āraṇyaka*, II, 3, 7.

131 That *soma* drops may stand for individualities is suggested in the *Pañcaviṁśa Brāhmaṇa*, VI, 9, 19.

132 Cf. Avalon, *Garland of Letters*, Ch. XIII. Eckhart, I, 464, "the boundary line between united and separated creatures. . . . There her aught abides, graven in a point." With "boundary line"; cf. again Islamic *jidāriyya*, the "murity" of the Outwardness contrasted with the Inwardness, see Nicholson, *Studies* . . . p. 95.

On the "point," cf. also Dante, *Paradiso*, XVII, 18, and XXVIII, 16 and 41-42, "*il punto, a cui tutti li tempi son presenti. . . . Un punto vidi che raggiava lume . . . Da qual punto depende il cielo, e tutti.*

133 It may be suggested that pre-Zoroastrian Magianism was faced by the possibility of a decay, similar to that which actually took place in Greece, by a humanisation and concomitant devitalisation of the older elemental, not "immortal" powers of the Year. Was Orphism a movement in Greece comparable to the Zoroastrian in Persia, or related to the Zoroastrian (cf. Harrison, *Themis*, 1927, pp. 465, 466), but which failed to avert an actual Olympian victory? In this case, the derogation of the *daevas* (even at the cost of introducing an appearance of duality, which in Manichaeism was still further developed) must be thought as Zoroaster's supreme achievement, and the main cause of the survival of Zoroastrianism as a living religion to-day. Olympian victory in Greece sealed the fate of Greek religion: Jesus repeated later what Zoroaster had accomplished in Persia, and Christianity has survived until now, when once more western religion stands in danger of rationalisation and replacement by a moral code (modern comparisons of Christianity and Stoicism are not without good reason).

In India it is true that the older designation "Asura" (Titan) gradually acquires an ill-omened sense, and that "Deva" (Olympian) takes its place as the preferred designation of the bright powers: but those who are thus made "Devas" (cf. Brown, W. N., *Proselytising the Asuras*, J.A.O.S., vol. 39, 1919) become Olympians only in name (except in the case of Indra), in fact they are the Titans of old. Thus, the Olympian victory is merely nominal; that the conquerors are really defeated by the conquered, corresponds to the defeat of "Aryan" by "indigenous" culture, again in all but name. It is true that Indra, who had been in Vedic times a power ranking with and competing with Varuṇa and Agni, is relegated, together with the once elemental Gandharvas and Apsarases, to an Olympian heaven of lasting pleasures: but Indra's spiritual importance, never comparable with that of Varuṇa, steadily decreases until in Buddhist and other post-Vedic literature he is hardly more than a literary figure and *deus ex machina*. Thus in India the danger of Olympianism seems to have passed without a definite crisis. The post-Vedic development is devotional rather than rationalistic. Viṣṇu and Śiva, though now somewhat more personally conceived, inherit directly from their Vedic prototypes. Śiva's drinking of the venom produced at the Churning of the Ocean and his iconography alone suffice to reveal him as a living God: and if Lakṣmī is sometimes little more than a figure of rhetoric, that is never true of Durgā. If Viṣṇu was ever in danger, that was precluded by the doctrine of his incarnations and passions, above all by his *avataraṇa* as Kṛṣṇa.

134 The notion of *phthonos* (see next note) first appears in *Bṛhadāraṇyaka Up.*, I, 4, 10.

NOTES

135 The development of Indra, the only one of the Vedic Angels to be completely humanized in later times, corresponds exactly to that of the Olympian deities in Greece, who renouncing the ceaseless activity, processions and recessions of the older Daimones of the Year, would be *athanatos* = *amṛta*, undying and immutable, whereby in fact they pass out of existence without achieving non-existence. In India it is realised clearly enough that Indra and his likes must be reborn as mortals before they can achieve or realise the non-existence, the true and absolute im-mortality of the Self. To all appearance Vedic *amṛtatva*, "not-dyingness," is equivalent to *dīrgham āyu*, "full length of days," and not to an absolute immortality, such as could only be predicated of those who are not "born"; that Agni himself is *nava navo jayamāna*, "born again and again," *bhūrijanma*, "of many births," necessarily involves that he also dies again and again (cf. *prajāyai mṛtyave*, of the Sun, in X, 72, 9) and this must apply *a fortiori* to all other "born" Angels, who are his "parts" and "powers." That Indra is an Angel jealous of his throne is an especially striking aspect of the psychological parallel: for it is precisely the Olympian gods who "begrudge a man a glory that may pale their own splendour," whereas "to the mystery-god Dionysos *phthonos* is unknown" (Harrison, *Themis*, p. 469). Hence the spiritual necessity for the defeat and displacement of Indra by Kṛṣṇa in the Govardhanadhara episode of the *Bhāgavata Purāṇa*, and the Buddhist emphasis on the relative worthlessness of a life in Indra's heaven.

Cf. Jeremias, *Der Kosmos von Sumer*, p. 9: "Im äonischen Kreislauf der das Weltgeschick ausmacht, kann die anti-polarische Strömung so stark wirksam werden, dass die gesamte stoffliche Welt von ihr durchimpft zu sein scheint, so dass man den geistigen Führer der Gegenschöpfung der 'Fürsten dieser Welt' nennen kann, was er in Wirklichkeit nie ist. Dann erscheint die wirkliche Welt als die böse Welt schlechthin und Erlösung wird zur 'Überwindung der Welt.'"

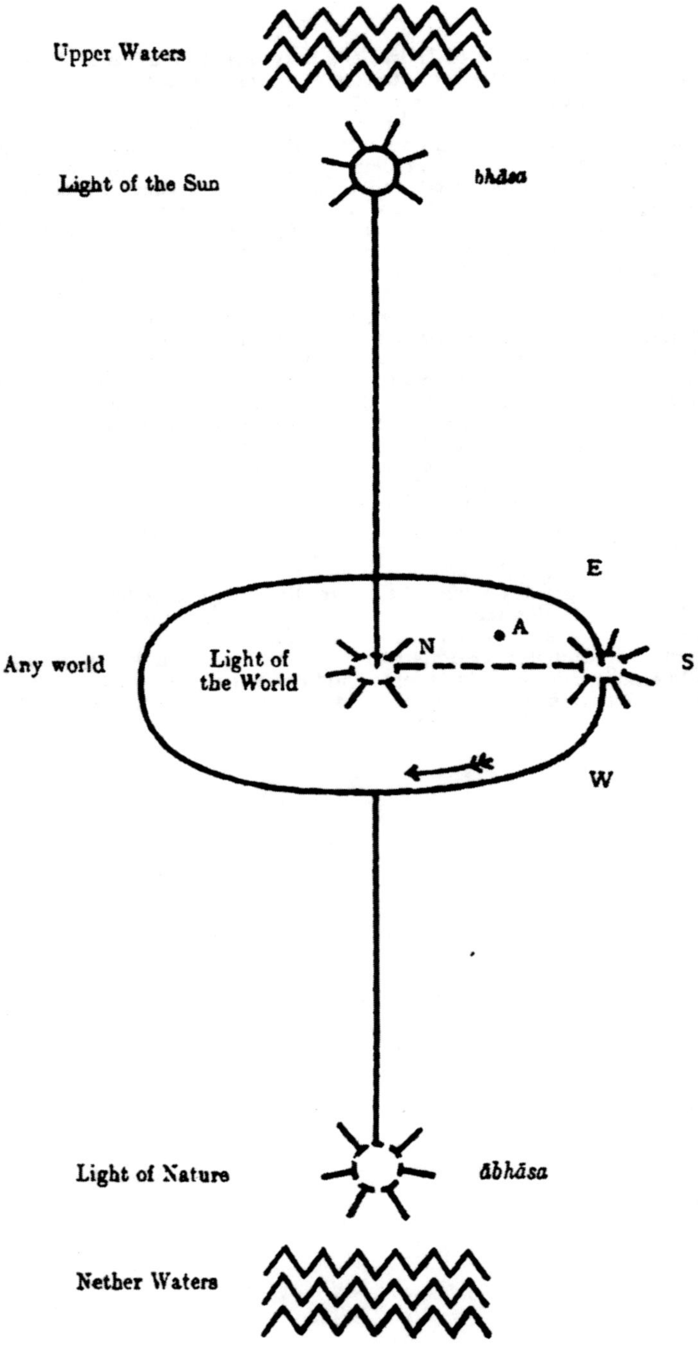
Upper Waters
Light of the Sun
bhāsa
E
A
N
Any world
Light of
the World
S
W
Light of Nature
ābhāsa
Nether Waters

APPENDIX

The Apparent Movement of the Sun as discussed in Note 65

The spiritual cosmology of the *Chāndogya Up.*, III, 6-11, where the Sun is said to rise successively in the East, South, West, North, and Zenith, and finally risen in the Centre to rise and set no more, these orientations corresponding to the types Vasu, Rudra, Āditya, Marut, Sādhya (= Muni), and Gnostic (*ya etamevaṁ brahmô-paniṣadaṁ veda*), may be better understood if presented in the form of a diagram, the formulation of the diagram in accordance with universal tradition being taken for granted. Here the circle, through the centre of which passes the vertical Axis of the Universe, represents a given World-Wheel, let us say that of the corporeal* mode of existence, as known to us here and now. Let "A" represent the "position" of any individual on this plane of experience, which position will be in the "middle space" (*rajas*) between the centre (Heaven, Essence, *sattva*) and the circumference (Earth, Substance, *tamas*). From the familiar correlation Devayāna, "by the North," and Pitṛyāna, "by the South," and other sources, we know that from the point of view of such an individual, "North" represents the centre, "South" that of the circumference. The revolution of the Wheel being sunwise, East and West will be in the directions indicated by the diagram. The spiritual condition of the individual can be indicated in such a diagram in two ways, (1) by his distance from the centre, and (2) by

* The vertical Axis is also the trunk of the Tree of Life, and every radius or spoke of every World-Wheel a branch of the Tree, and amongst these branches are the "nests" of individual conscience.

the direction in which he "faces." Now the normal course (*gati*) of spiritual experience is in the first place centrifigual (*pravṛtta*, lit. "extro-vert"), affirmative, extensive, and in the second centripetal (*nivṛtta*, lit. "retro-vert"), re-formative, intensive. The affirmative movement will involve a removal from and a turning away from the centre, the individual "facing East," i.e. forward with respect to the movement of the Wheel, and for him the Sun "rises in the East": actually, the light he sees is compounded of the "Light of Heaven" and the "Light of Nature" (the "Light of Nature" being the reflection, *ābhāsa*, at the circumference, of the "Light of Heaven" at the centre). Now this affirmative movement proceeds, until the individual attains a maximum distance from the centre, and "faces South": he sees then only the "Light of Nature," for him the Sun "rises in the South." That is the night and Winter solstice of his spiritual life. That the Sun sets in the "North" corresponds to the point of view of the sensual and materially scientific man whose "realities" must be "facts," and for whom "ideas" are "mere abstractions," observation being his "enlightenment," vision his "night"; cf. *Bhagavad Gītā*, II, 69, "In what is 'night' to all existences, therein the tempered conscience is awake; and in what existences are 'wakeful,' is 'night' for the Muni who 'sees' indeed."

Turning toward the centre, the conscience moves toward the centre, facing also West, which is at the same time "backward" with respect to the movement of the Wheel; for him the Sun "rises in the West"; again he sees a "Light" compounded of the Light of Nature and of the Light of Heaven. That the light of the Sun shines now out of the West is inasmuch as the individual now realises his true end, and that Life Eternal (timeless) is theirs only who can die to things temporal, "He that would save his life, let him lose it." Finally he comes to stand near to the centre of the Wheel, the centre of his own being, and "faces North," then indeed the Sun "rises in the North," he sees only the Light of Heaven, the Light of Nature is in the south behind him.

Observe, of course, that the direction of the rising Sun (whether in the East, South, West, or North "spiritually") is always spoken of as "East" (le Levant, l'Orient) empirically (all our images being derived from sensible experience): hence when the Bodhisattva takes his seat upon the Adamantine Throne, about to realise the Great Awakening, he is said to face the "East," that is locally with respect to his actual séance at Gayā, but spiritually "North." In the same way are to be explained the various orientations of temples, normally, for example, we should expect that the worshipper must enter from the South, the Devayāna (Chinese Shên-tao, Japanese Shinto) which leads directly to the shrine (*garbha*) running from South to North; but if the image worshipped be *rājasika*, the orientation may be actually East or West, and if the image be *tamāsika*, entrance must be from the North.

Further, the four stages of the course as described above correspond to Spring, Summer, Autumn, Winter in *pratyakṣa, adhyâtma* sequence, or Autumn, Winter (*ut supra*), Spring, and Summer in *parokṣa, adhidaivata* sequence: similarly, to Infancy, Youth, Maturity, and Age in our corporeal parlance, that is to Maturity, Age, Youth, and Infancy, spiritually, cf. *pāṇḍityaṁ nirvidya bālyena tiṣthâset*, "putting aside learning, let him abide in innocence" (*Bṛhadāraṇyaka Up.*, III, 5†): and also to the four *aśrāmas* in the Brahmanical map of life.

When now the conscience is wholly retroverted, centred

* For the inversion of meaning, cf. *Ṛg Veda*, I, 164, 19, "Those that come hitherward (*arvañc*), they (viz. the Angels) call 'departing' (*parācaḥ*)."

† Almost literally equivalent to the words of Jesous, "Except ye become again as little children"; and of Paulos, *Corinthians*, I, 3, 18, "If anyone amongst you thinketh himself to be wise in the world, let him become as one ungrown, that he may be wise indeed."

within itself and within the Nave of the World-Wheel, the individual becomes a Sādhya, "*geworden was er ist,*" Sukṛtàtman, "Per-fected self," Jīvanmukta, "set free while yet existent on a given plane of being," *bālyaṁ ca pāṇḍityaṁca nirvidya atha muniḥ*, "putting aside innocence and learning both, then is he a Muni," (*Bṛhadāraṇyaka Up.*, III, 5). The conscience that had been "Wakeful" (*jagrat*) is now "Fast Asleep" (*suṣupta*) in terms of mortal understanding, but angelically speaking "Wide Awake" (*prabuddha*). The Buddha Śākya-Muni, seated upon his adamantine throne at the navel of the earth, which throne is based upon the axial column that extends from nethermost to uppermost, is a case in point. There, as the Buddhist texts affirm, "all former Munis have taken their seat," being now *saṁbuddha*, "Wide Awake." This is indeed the station of the Son of Man and the Son of God, however designated. *Puruṣa mahā taha adhika virājai*, "There the Great Person shines resplendent" (Kabīr), having now become the Light of the World, which "previous" to his Enlightenment, Transfiguration, or Ascension (in fact, he is no longer limited by concepts of "before" or "after") had seemed to be the Light of Heaven, the very Supernal Sun. Clothed with the Sun, he is invisible to mortal eyes, as Muni, "Silent," inaudible to corporeal ears, his appearance in the world can be only by way of *avatarana* "descent," and in an "appointed" (*nirmāta*) body; "I am the Silence of the Hidden" (*mauna guhyānām*, *Bhagavad Gītā*, X, 38).

In Vasubandhu's *Abhidharmakośa*, II, 42-44, and *Triṁśikāvijñapti*, the same ideas are expressed somewhat differently. The conscience of one who is still on the mundane path (*laukika mārga*) remains "general" or "demotic" (*pṛthak*), he can attain only to the "encountering of non-ideation" (*asaṁjñisamāpatti*), corresponding to "childishness" or "innocence" (*bālya*) above; and the demotic Wayfarer may mistake this heavenly station for true deliverance (*niḥsaraṇa*).* This is in fact a state of "passive integration," inasmuch as it is reached "by the efficacy of the path" (*mārgabalena labhyatvāt, Abhidharmakośa*, VI, 34); a salvation in the religious or mystical, not the metaphysical sense. The demotic conscience, even of a Saint or Bodhisattva, is arrested at this level of understanding, by a latent residue of ideal affectibility; a return to consciousness is always imminent.

Proceeding now, however, as the Saint or Bodhisattva may, on the "noble" or "transmundane" path (*ārya mārga, lokôttara mārga*), the Wayfarer, now an "aristocrat" or "nobleman" (*ārya*), oversteps the mere "suppression of intellection" and reaches the "place of neither ideation nor non-ideation" (*naivasaṁjñānâsaṁjñānâyatana*), corresponding to "neither learning nor innocence," above; which place, viz. the highest level of non-aspectual (*arūpya*) being, is also called the "summit of being," *bhavâgra*. Then is he a Comprehensor, Vidvān, Muni, Sādhya, Jina, *prabuddha, saṁbuddha*.

As he is in himself, Sādhya, etc., his "position" on the Axis of the Universe makes him free of its entire extension; that is, he may operate on all or any of the indefinitely numerous planes of being that revolve in the "middle space" about this Axis, "he goes up and down these worlds, eating what he desires, assuming what aspect he will," *Taittirīya Up.*, III, 10, 5. At the same time it is evident that from the point of view of any or every station on the Axis the source of Light, Oriens, East,

* *Nirvāṇa*, rebirth in a Buddha Paradise (=a Brahma-world), though it may be mistaken for the last end, is not yet in fact an absolute extinction (*parinirvāṇa*), as is explained in the *Saddharma Puṇḍarīka*, V, 74, "this is a resting place (*viśrāma*), not a return (*nirvṛti*)," and *ibid.*, XV, 21, "I display return who am not myself returned (*anirvṛto nirvṛta darśayāmi*)," cf. Eckhart's "It is God's full intention that we should become what he is not." As also in the *Chāndogya Up.*, III, 13, 7, "There is a light that shines beyond this heaven (Brahma-world), at the back of everything, and that too shines within us," cf. *Ṛg Veda*, VI, 9, 5, "a steady Light set up to be seen . . . , and set within the heart" and *ibid.*, IV, 58, "within the Sea, the Heart, and living things," all which corresponds to the Buddhist doctrine of the *bodhicitta*.

is seen " above," the Supernal Sun "rises in the zenith," and its obscuration is " below," it " sets in the Nadir " ; and this must and will be maintained " so long as " any awareness of duality, even conscience of Sonship in relation, persists in him, whatever be the level of manifestation. That " so long as " will be figuratively speaking, during the " hundred years " of Brahmā's life, until the end of time. Only when all conscience of duality has passed away, *amaunaṁ ca maunaṁ ca nirvidya atha brāhmaṇaḥ*, " laying aside both manifestation and non-manifestation, then is he Brāhmaṇa,"* *brahmavid*, " knowing the Brahman in identity," *Bṛhādaraṇyaka Up.*, III, 5. Then the Axis of the Universe is contracted to a point, that point *al cui la prima rota va dintorno*, all forms subsisting in a single form ; then only is the Supernal Sun " forever risen, there is no more rising and setting, He is verily One (*ekata*), in the Middle Place "† (*madhye sthāne* = *nābhā amṛtasya*, " in the navel of non-mortality "), " without duality," *advaita*.

The applications of a diagram such as that here illustrated are indefinitely numerous. For example, the line extending from the Southern Sun in the world, to the central Light of the World, and continuously thence by a right turn upward to the Supernal Sun, represents that one amongst the many paths that Agni knows, which leads through the Solar Gateway of the Worlds (*loka-dvāra*, cf. JUB. 1, 3 and John x, 1-18) to the Empyrean (*parama vyoman*), the Motionless Pleroma. Agni being the Herdsman of the Flocks, who wanders in the worlds unfalteringly, and stands way-wise at the cross-roads (*Ṛg Veda*, I, 164, 31 ; X, 5, 6 ; X, 19 ; and X, 177, 3). " There is no side path here in the world " (*Maitri Up.*,

* For this special use of the word *brāhmaṇa*, cf. in *Ṛg Veda*, X, 71, 11, *brahmā*, " the Brahman," viz., that one of the four sacrificial priests who *vadati jātavidyām*, " utters the lore of genesis " ; Sāyaṇa's comment being *brahma hi sarvaṁ védituṁ yogyā bhavati khalu*, " ' Brahman ' refers to the one associated in that he knows everything but is merely present." Hence Agni's epithet, *Jātavedas*.

† Or " Place Within," i.e., *guhā nihitam*, *antarbhūtasya khe*.

VI, 30) no Ray or Way that leads from any position in the world directly to the Supernal Sun: the Supernal Sun is only visible from the centre in the world, a centre without "position" in space, but where is the Light of the World, the Eye of the World, Buddhist *cakkhuṁ loke*. In other words, "it is through the midst of the Supernal Sun that one escapes" (*ādityaṁ samayā atimucyate*, JUB., I, 3; "No man cometh to the Father but through Me."

In a more detailed representation, the number of "wheels" or "circles" (*cakra*) must be indefinitely increased. In particular, one great circle passes through the Supernal Sun and its reflection in the Nether Waters, this circle marking out the World or Universe in its entirety, its revolution being the Brahmâṇḍa; and on the other hand, the individual conscience "A" must be represented by yet another circle, in a plane at right angles to that in which the conscience subsists, each and all of such worlds being in the image of (*anurūpam*) of the other. In the individual "world" there will be seen again reflected Suns, one central, virtually "without position," but "actually" situated at the point of intersection with the solar ray in the world already spoken of, and represented by the dotted line: the other peripheral. Those central and peripheral "Suns" of the individual conscience are the individual's "Inner Light" and "Light of Nature." Looking within the individual sees this Inner Light, "risen in the North"; and being centred therein, he has entered upon the general "Way" which is represented by the dotted line in the diagram. That the direction of this "Way" stands at right angles to that of his former "axis," corresponds to that *rectification** of personality which is commonly

* Cf. *Kauṣītaki Brāhmaṇa*, VII, 6, where the Zenith is said to have been "first discerned" by Aditi, and it is because Aditi, whose "Liberty" (*adititva*) is from all bonds, is thus of the Zenith, that all things, plants, trees, men, and fire "stand upright," the "rectitude" of things being their "aspiration."

spoken of as "conversion" and "regeneration" ("Except a man be born again, he cannot see the Kingdom of God"). Along this new-won Way he must proceed until he reaches and is centred in the Light of the World* ; then for the first time he sees directly, *sâkṣāt aparokṣāt*, the Supernal Sun, "risen in the Zenith," "whose Face is Fire" (*Ṛg Veda*, VII, 88, 2)—*per tal modo che ciò ch'io dice è un semplice lume, Paradiso*, XXXIII, 90.

On the other hand, with regard to procession, inasmuch as the extension of any world lies in a plane at right angles to the axis of the universe (cf. JUB., I, 29, *raśmi asumaya . . . tiraṇ pratiṣṭhataḥ*) any coming into existence is represented by a branching outwards horizontally from the trunk of the Tree of Life or vertical of the Cross. The Several Angels are therefore said to be "born transversely, from the side" (*Ṛg Veda*, IV, 18, 1-2) and this image survives in the Buddhist legend of the birth of Siddhârtha from Māyādevī's side.

* "Thereof is he the Splendour (*śri*), the Self (*ātman*) arisen from the Sea (*samudrūḍha*), viz. yonder Supernal Sun (*āditya*)," *JUB.*, III, 3.